CHAKRAS FOR BEGINNERS

The Updated Guide to Balance your Chakras with Chakra Healing, Mindfulness and Morning Meditation

Mindfulness Journey

publisher for any reparation, damages, or monetary loss due to the information herein, either directly or indirectly.

Respective authors own all copyrights not held by the publisher.

The information herein is offered for informational purposes solely, and is universal as so. The presentation of the information is without contract or any type of guarantee assurance.

The trademarks that are used are without any consent, and the publication of the trademark is without permission or backing by the trademark owner. All trademarks and brands within this book are for clarifying purposes only and are the owned by the owners themselves, not affiliated with this document.

Disclaimer

All erudition contained in this book is given for informational and educational purposes only. The author is not in any way accountable for any results or outcomes that emanate from using this material. Constructive attempts have been made to provide information that is both accurate and effective, but the author is not bound for the accuracy or use/misuse of this information.

Foreword

First, I will like to thank you for taking the first step of trusting me and deciding to purchase/read this life-transforming eBook. Thanks for spending your time and resources on this material.

I can assure you of exact results if you will diligently follow the exact blueprint, I lay bare in the information manual you are currently reading. It has transformed lives, and I strongly believe it will equally transform your own life too.

All the information I presented in this "Do It Yourself" book is easy to digest and practice.

PAGE INTENTIONALLY LEFT BLANK

Table of Contents

INTRODUCTION

In this book, I'll present the idea of chakras so you can get a good understanding on your energy centers. This is an extraordinary place to start in case you're new to chakras and need a beginner level review. In case you're prepared to plunge into increasingly deeper philosophies for each chakra, flip ahead to where the detailed chakra diagrams are discussed (Chapter). In case you're interested to find out about the different ways by which individuals work with chakras—from meditation to yoga to gem healing—peruse the "Tackling Your Chakra Power" aspect of this book.

It is important to note that your chakras are a significant driving component in each part of your daily life. This book also addresses basic unbalanced characteristics that reflect on physical, mental, emotional, and psychological levels, and it offers supportive methods to start healing these irregular characteristics, each chakra in turn. To become familiar with which of your chakras may need balancing, Peruse and deeply examine the book for the indications or diseases with which you might be battling. When you've identifies which chakra or chakras you'd like to adjust or recuperate, start working through the chakra healing strategies discussed in this book.

As you expect to address the question "What is a chakra?" it's critical to take a look at the verifiable causes of the chakras. The idea linked to early Hinduism and Buddhism. Hinduism specifically records up to seven chakras, but Buddhism makes reference to only five. The derivation of the word chakra originates from old Hindu writings, where it is utilized to signify "wheel." It is additionally said to identify with the Greek word "Kuklos," and the Anglo-Saxon word "hveohl." These all assign a wheel or something to that effect. These regular starting points all accentuate the interconnected and continually moving nature of the chakras.

Do chakras really exist? Think about the fact that the history of chakra, unmistakably represents the life span and viability of chakra-based conventions. These real central centers have been the subject of meditations, breathing processes, and mantras, all of which means to utilize the chakras to identify and address physical and mental issues. However, you may have found the idea of chakras perplexing. Or, on the other hand, you have not exactly understood what spot it might have in your life. Things being what they are, everybody can work with chakras, not simply specialists. Every one of these powerful energy centers are one of a kind vibsrational recurrences. Along these lines, even a basic understanding of the seven chakras can upgrade your life in astounding ways.

CHAPTER ONE

What Are Chakras?

You are already acquainted with your physical body. You know how it feels to flex or broaden a zone of your body; that your muscles are connected to your bones; that your nerves signal to your appendages, abdomen, and head; and that what you eat and drink influences your wellbeing. In these ways, you would already be able to perceive how parts of your physical being are connected with one another and how your perceptions – through touch, smell, taste, sight, and hearing – inform one another, making your environment.

In any case, your physical body isn't the main body you have. Regardless of whether you're considering chakras or quantum material science, you come to discover that everything is energy, with its own vibrational recurrence. From the most basic particles that make our cells, organs, bones, muscles, and actual systems to the most far reaching planet in the close planetary system, everything is comprised of energy. What's more, that energy has numerous names: qi, ki, chi, prana, mana, Odic power, bioplasm, and life power energy, among many others.

The energy body is the human energy field that reaches out past the physical body. Much as your physical body comprises of numerous layers—your sensory system, musculature, and skeletal system—with multifaceted, encompassing capacities, your energy body also comprises of many interfacing layers. Like your physical body, each layer fills a particular need and the layers work together as one. Together, the layers of your energy body are called your aura. Your aura links with your physical body as well as your energy centers, or chakras.

The word chakra is from the Sanskrit word cakra, signifying "wheel." It was first referenced in the Vedas, old Hindu messages that date to around 1,500 BCE. From time unknown, numerous societies—including the Egyptians, Hindus, Chinese, Sufis, Zarathustrians, Greeks, Native Americans, Incas, and the Mayans, among others—have all realized these energy centers, or the chakra system, to be an impression of the normal law that exists inside the universe and an entwined partner to our physical selves. Chakras are energy vortexes that exist inside every one of us. These energy vortexes transport energy from the universe around you into your atmosphere and body, as well as between the physical body and the layers of your aura. You can think about your chakra system as like a psychological circulation system. Blood conveys oxygen, supplements, and hormones all through the body; directs and balance the body; and secures the body by expelling waste items and dealing when the body is hurt. Much similarly, your circulation system connects and supports your numerous other physical systems, your chakra system links and supports your physical self and your energy self.

Every single living thing—people, creatures, plants, trees, even the Earth—have a chakra system, a living arrangement of energy vortexes, that exists inside them. There are seven significant chakras in the body, as well as a few minor ones. Each is related to explicit tissues and organs, physical capacities and dysfunctions, and emotional, mental, and psychological issues. We'll get into more particulars about each later in this book.

At the point when we connect with the energy inside our chakras, we link with ourselves all the more completely, and figure out how to recuperate ourselves on all levels, experiencing genuine all-encompassing healing. This is the reason care-based practices, for example, meditation, help connect the mind with body and soul, why certain physical exercises can help clear your head and feel increasingly focused, and why developing your soul recovers your brain and body. It is altogether connected.

Feel your Chakras

To connect with your energy, hold your hands one inch apart, palms facing one another. Get acquainted with the light and energy trade between your hands (our hands contain minor chakras). Separate your hands somewhat, "loosening up" the energy between your palms. At that point, unite them once more, consolidating your energy. Repeat a couple of times, playing with the energy between the palms of your hands. Try not to stress if you don't appear to feel anything from the onset.

Relax, clear your mind, and proceed with staying open and on top of yourself. As you become increasingly acquainted with your energy, you won't just have the opportunity to see the glow of your hands (which will increase, in any event, when your hands are more far apart), yet additionally, a slight energy charge between them. With time and persistence, you'll have the opportunity to feel this charge all the more firmly, in any event, when you separate your hands further apart.

You can feel your major chakras, as well. For example, to feel your heart chakra, place two hands at the focal point of your chest. Take a moderate constant breath through your nose. Feel the glow and internal shine underneath your hands. You are not just feeling your pulse, or the coursing of your blood, but also the feeling of your heart chakra extending.

Feel it? Congrats, you are currently connecting with your chakras! If you don't feel anything as yet, don't stress. With time and practice, your affectability will increase.

The Power of Chakras to Heal

Information of chakras for healing and edification is ancient knowledge — wisdom that has been known in numerous ancient societies for quite a long time. Later interest in chakras is on the grounds that we are beginning to feel, to an ever-increasing extent, that concentrating exclusively on our physical wellbeing isn't bringing us complete health. Regardless of the numerous achievements of modern medicine, something still feels absent or "off," despite the fact that we can't exactly put our finger on it.

As the daughter of a Western doctor, I am completely mindful of Western medication's commitments to wellbeing, and value its worth. I grew up perusing my dad's medicinal references and discovered that the human body is entirely stunning. All things being equal, I accept individuals are beginning to understand that some way or another—regardless of whether we don't get it—different components may impact our present wellbeing challenges.

Imagine a scenario in which you discovered that a considerable amount of the physical indications we experience (excepting occasions like car crashes and other direct physical injury) could be avoided, basically on the grounds that huge numbers of our physical side effects are expressions of what hasn't been tended to in the energy body.

Enter the Chakras

When our chakras are in balance, our lives are in complete agreement and our wellbeing is great. In the event that a chakra gets blocked, we will in the long run experience emotional trouble or sickness. Since everything is energy, when we mend and keep up our energy body's wellbeing—through modalities like acupuncture, Reiki, meditation, yoga, and qi gong, among others—and settle on a better way of life and food choices, we really recover issues that may arise, before they show in the physical body.

Myths about Chakra Healing

Before we get into the varied aspects of the chakra system, I need to dispel a few myths about chakra healing.

Myth 1: Chakra healing is an external activity.

Regardless of whether you get external healing help from an expert in your chakra healing venture, at last, you are the person who is the healer of you, not another person. This is something I generally tell my patients. Despite the fact that I may at times utilize the expression "healer" regarding what I do, healing is constantly an internal activity. While healing practitioners can direct you on your journey, we are each answerable for our very own healing.

Myth 2: Chakra healing is connected with a particular religion.

In spite of the fact that the first sources of the chakra system originated from sacred writings, chakra healing has since extended to arrive at a more far-reaching knowledge and practice, and is currently grasped by individuals from numerous different backgrounds. Developing chakra wellbeing has become a significant practice for some in a profound way and isn't related with religion.

Myth 3: Chakra healing is a type of satanic, or dull, custom.

Genuine chakra healing, done right, is a remarkable inverse of wicked. You are mixing light, mindfulness, and awareness into your body, mind, soul, and heart—all of which dispel darkness.

Chakra Healing Warnings

When engaging with healing your chakras, there are a couple of things you ought to recall as you start.

Be patient with yourself. I regularly find that the individuals who are simply beginning to connect with their chakras become upset with themselves rapidly. Regularly, they start to pass judgment on themselves as disappointments in the event that they don't see quick improvements. However, everybody is extraordinary, and everybody has their very own ideal course of events of their own development, and everything is going on precisely as it should, including your healing.

Chakra healing, regardless of whether it is being developed to address a particular issue or to accomplish edification, is an inward investigation, not an objective. Along these lines, similar to physical healing, chakra healing isn't something you can basically "accelerate." However, accepting healing treatments and different methods can get out active waste and bring your energy centers more into concordance. Change takes tolerance. Be sympathetic with yourself as you blossom.

Try not to propel yourself past what is agreeable, or power your energy. At the point when individuals are anxious to connect with their chakras, they regularly propel themselves past what is agreeable. However, you may, before long, experience cerebral pain (literally!). When you start feeling some opposition, enjoy a reprieve.

Find support from a healing practitioner when it's fundamental. You can achieve a great deal alone, however, some of the time, direction can be useful, particularly in the event that you have a feeling that you're reaching a stopping point in your healing venture, or the pain showed is influencing your personal satisfaction. If you choose to find support, ensure the practitioner is authorized or guaranteed in their methodology. Look at them completely before making an arrangement. Guarantee it'll be a solid match for you, and that you will have a sense of security.

How The Chakras Relate To Our Lives

We are taught that if we're angry, it's because something transpired that induced the feeling. But this is really in reverse. At the point when an upsetting event happens, such as, pain, sickness or annoyance within your system, or even an "outside" illness, by way of, losing a job or a connection, that circumstance is a feeling of being "resentful" which has been in the point within us more frequently than not, under our watchful mindfulness.

For example, what if your significant other or spouse requires separation and you're feeling angry. The event of your partner having a separation is the overall examination of part of you, which is "split" from another aspect of yourself – even a place in which you have separated from yourself.

How we experience being treated by another individual is a feeling of how we handle ourselves, which is the way we believe we all SHOULD be taken care of.

The Chakras might mimic this belief also, as there is no uncertainty in sun-based plexus and centre within this version, in the same way, the neck and the first two rhythms, to changing degrees. Each of the cells and organs from the areas of the human body identified as having all the chakras would similarly be affected.

CHAPTER TWO

Chakras Fundamentals

The chakra system is an antiquated system, known to numerous societies for a huge number of years. Chakra (articulated CHUK-ruh) implies wheel or hover in Sanskrit. In Tibetan Buddhism, the centers are called channel wheels. Taoist yoga is a mind-boggling belief dependent on the control and flow of these fundamental energies seen as vortexes.

Chakras are additionally called lotuses, which gives us some thought of the idea of the chakras. The lotus with its stunning blossoms sprouting on the outside of the water, under the light of the Sun (soul), has its underlying foundations covered in the sloppy dimness of the depths (the physical). Much the same as the lotus bloom, the chakras can be shut, in bud, opening or blooming, dynamic or lethargic.

The old western catalytic custom utilized the chakra system, with metals and planets being appointed to the chakras in an intricate arrangement of messages, which shaped the premise of the chemists' mission for profound change. With the decrease of catalytic expressions, learning of the chakras obscured further. Interest in the chakras reappeared in the west with the presence of the Theosophy development in the mid-twentieth century.

The chakra system is a lively information stockpiling system, particularly like a PC, which numerous healers feel or see. It is the psychological link between the physical body, through the nervous system, our soul body, and the universe. The nervous system is our physical link, communicating with all parts of the physical, presenting information to and getting from the chakras. The chakras work as transmitters of energy, starting with one level then onto the next, conveying qi or prana to the physical body.

Although there many minor chakras in the body and in our minds, it is perceived that there are seven (7) significant chakras between the crotch and top of the head, with two (2) others that are vital, found around 18 inches over the crown of the head, known as the Soul Star, the Earth Star found roughly 18 inches underneath the feet. There are contrasts of supposition with respect to where a portion of the minor chakras are. I work with and balance 16 significant chakras, from the Earth Star right to the Monad – Divine connection – some of which are not perceived by different healers or systems, making my healing work novel.

Individual experience is a fundamental part of western acknowledgment for everything. Our "I'll trust it when I see it" disorder, confines humankind's multi-tactile encounters. There are many detailed frequencies, however. Take for example individuals who have had physical pain, in the heart for instance, with no physiological explanation found, much after broad medicinal testing. At the point when these individuals proceeded to have a precious stone healing and chakra balance, the healer saw that their pain as connected with previous existence damage and the pain settled after the rebalance. Numerous healers accept that physical ailments have their root in mental and emotional imbalances, and so as to recuperate the physical body, one should also address the psychological and emotional bodies too.

Every last one of the ordinarily perceived seven chakras compares to a physical system and its related tissues and organs. Sound, colors, and crystals are appointed to each chakra; however, the colors and elements of each chakra change fairly as indicated by various conventions.

The First Chakra: Base Chakra situated at the region of the coccyx at the base of the spine, identifies with the adrenals, internal organs, and rectum. It imparts the duty of the kidneys to the second chakra. This chakra is known as the kundalini or snake's fire; life power for endurance, life or "passing" fight, family personality, holding, and dedication. The root chakra's expression of energy is legitimately identified with an individual's nature of wellbeing. The inestimable fire that anticipates discharge lies torpid until the higher self can appropriately use the strength of its ethereal energy source on physical and psychological levels of life. The exercise of the first chakra is that of oneness instead of detachment. Its shading is red. Crystals are Garnet, Black Tourmaline, Dravite, Black Onyx, Smokey Quartz, and Obsidian. Its Note is center C.

The Second Chakra: Sacral Chakra is found halfway between abdomen and navel (a few customs see it at the navel) and identifies with the testicles, prostate, and ovaries. The pelvis is the physical portrayal of the Void and The Goddess. This is the place the Inner Feminine/Goddess Self struggles. It is the innovative focus and identifies with eroticism as well as sexuality, influence (individual influence when it is in balance, and ego domination when it is unequal) and cash or wealth, the capacity to make and go out on a limb, fight or flight, flexibility, tirelessness, and money related intuition. This at that point is our innovative focus, the seat of our energy and our sexuality – being agreeable in our body as a lady or man. Shadow viewpoints: disempowering/controlling or utilizing others for your very own desires. Shading: orange; Note: D; Crystals: Amber, Tiger Eye, and Carnelian.

The Third Chakra: Solar Plexus Chakra identifies with the pancreas, liver, gallbladder, stomach, spleen, and assimilation. This is the place our uncertain feelings are put away and is subsequently where we "digest" our feelings, or not! This chakra identifies with resolve, confidence, self-control, aspiration, mental fortitude, liberality, morals and senses, dignity and respecting of self. Shadow perspectives: giving endlessly close to home intensity of decision out of a requirement for endorsement; narcissistic conduct. Shading: yellow; Note: E; Crystals: Citrine, Sunstone, and Lemon Chrysophrase.

The Fourth Chakra: Heart Chakra is situated in the focal point of the chest identifies with the thymus glands and heart. This is simply the chakra of affection and others, sympathy and absolution. Shadow perspectives: desire, misery, disdain, and the failure to forgive. Shading: a blend of pink, for self-esteem, and green, for affection for other people. We should initially cherish ourselves before we can adore another; Note: F; Crystals: Rose Quartz, Green Aventurine, Amazonite, and Chrysophrase.

The Fifth Chakra: Throat Chakra is situated at the base of the throat, identifies with the thyroid and parathyroid glands and the neck. It identifies with our capacity to speak our truth and confide in ourselves and is the place we permit love into our lives. It is the place we apply our will over others or give our capacity/will away to other people. This is simply the focal point of confidence, information, individual authority, and the capacity to keep your promise. Shadow viewpoints: an over the top need to control connections and occasions. Shading: blue; Note: G; Crystals: Larimar, Blue Lace Agate, Lapis, Aquamarine, Azurite/Malachite, and Gem Silica.

The Sixth: Brow Chakra is regularly called the third eye, is situated between and somewhat over the eye brows. It identifies with the pineal organ and psychological vision, and the capacity to verbalize vision and motivation. Shadow viewpoints: characterizing reality in self-serving ways. Shading: purple; Note: A; Crystals: Amethyst, Sugilite, Kyanite, and Azurite.

The Seventh Chakra: Crown Chakra is situated at the highest point of the head and can be found by "engaging" a line up from the highest point of the ears and straight up from the tip of the nose. It identifies with the pituitary organ and is our immediate connection with soul and higher awareness. This is the focal point of confidence in the Divine as well as in inward direction, understanding into healing and dedication to the Divine. Shadow viewpoint: the need to know why things occur as they do, which makes you live before. Shading: white; Note: B; Crystal: Clear Quartz, Selenite, and Indicolite (Blue) Quartz.

I got the accompanying information from the Divine in a healing session year back. As I have worked with these chakras, my understanding of them has developed. Individuals are to some degree acquainted with the eighth chakra, otherwise called the Soul Star or Interpersonal Chakra. Less is thought about charkas nine through twelve. Information fluctuates with regards to the higher measurements. That is on the grounds that individuals are on various degrees of mindfulness or hold diverse vibrational levels. You can just observe reality dependent on where you are looking from at the time.

The 5 Higher Chakras, 8 - 12 These five higher charkas were separated ages prior and are presently being reconnected through our opening to Spirit. The process can be sped up through an Ascension Initiation. The shades of the higher charkas shift from individual to individual and is subject to your individual reason or capacity as soul. Crystals: Herkimer and Tibetan Diamonds, twofold ended Clear Quartz, Selenite,

Indicolite (Blue Tourmaline in Quartz), Moldavite, Cavansite, Apophyllite, and Prehnite.

The Eighth Chakra: Soul Star otherwise called the Transpersonal chakra, is around 18 inches over the head. This is the inside that holds every one of our agreements and understandings identified with this lifetime, karmic connections, etc. An individual's Soul Star covers with that of the individuals they've had long haul connections or sexual experiences with, and they don't totally disengage without anyone else, despite the fact that the couple may part physically. It's significant, in this way, to have the option to clear each one of those former relationship contracts, so as to clear a path for new potential connections to come to you all the more effectively, or to clear a pathway for the relationship of your current, supporting it to develop all the more completely. The eighth chakra is also the focal point of separation, remaining right now, unequivocal trust, acknowledgment of instinctive direction and the capacity to observe deception. It is the focal point of higher wisdom. It denotes the domain where the individual soul converges with the Universal Mind. It additionally denotes the point where the spirit shows into matter, into the individual energy body. Note: C.

The Ninth Chakra: Intergalactic Gateway to the Divine and the Blueprint for this manifestation and our Higher Emotional Center. This is the place we hold all the information identified with who we will be and are, in this present manifestation - our eye shading, hair shading, different highlights, character attributes, and what we will be/do in this lifetime. This information turns into our DNA. We pick this before we come into this manifestation. In a healing, the Blueprint may seem divided, harmed or broken, split, shattered, dissipated or even dispelled. I worked with one lady who was very discouraged and I had a feeling that she would not like to be here. She affirmed this when I asked her. Her diagram really seemed dispelled or dissipated and I accept she would have attempted to leave by one way or another if she hadn't had the session with me. She burst into tears when I asked that another outline be made, and she felt totally extraordinary after the session. Specifically, she had a tremendous release when I cleared her ninth and eleventh chakras. Note: D.

The Tenth Chakra: Interdimensional Gateway to the Divine is the door to the various encounters (and measurements) we've had all through the universe. This chakra is the place the spirit pieces itself and dissipates itself all through the universe, requiring "recovery." When all angles are recovered, the individual has full access to all the unending potential outcomes of who they've been and are- - their "all-inclusive prime examples," for need of a superior term. By bringing the quintessence of those perspectives or soul sections into one chakra, it enables us to work with every one of our gifts and capacities. Many people just approach somewhere in the range of one and ten of their general prime examples, and that is very constraining on the grounds that we really have a boundless number. Note: E.

The Eleventh chakra: Universal Gateway to the Divine is the place duality starts, in a manner of speaking. It is the "field of cover" between Light and Dark, and is the place we have all agreements and understandings, having a place with our spirit, though the eighth chakra is this present manifestation's agreements and understandings. Clearing the eleventh chakra is significant in bringing an individual into balance and enabling them to have full access to their Divinity. I find that squares in the eleventh chakra are well on the way to meddle with our Divine connection. This is the place our agreements with the mysterious, dark enchantment, and the Abyss are held. There is a part of ourselves that have encountered the shadow, since that is a piece of the Soul's adventure to investigate Light and Dark, Order and Chaos. Part of the Divine plan for us is to encounter Duality – Light and Dark and every one of the beams of the rainbow in the middle. Some of the time I find that this chakra is very imbalanced and may require a generous imbuement of love, and maybe "another" chakra make by required. At the point when I clear with this chakra, individuals frequently experience a moment move, and they remark that they all of a sudden feel extraordinary, progressively connected with the Divine. Note: F

The Twelfth charka: Monadic Soul Level completing the five higher charkas is the twelfth chakra or the Monad is viewed as the individualized Spirit-Spark of the Divine and is frequently called the "I am Presence." The Monad is regularly viewed as the Ascended Pro Level of the Soul. Every Monad or Spirit-Spark makes and is isolated into 12 sets of Souls. Each pair are known as Twin Flames. The Monad is regularly viewed as the Ascended Pro or Spirit level of Soul. When being cleared I see the individual's Twin Flame as well as their Divine Ray - their own kind of the Divine, in shading recurrence, which is their "work" as Spirit.

Here is the Blueprint of the Soul, the Soul's Twin Flame- - twin-self or mirror inverse. Sporadically I see the spirits of other critical connections here. It's where there is no separation between the Monad and the Divine. Regularly, I see that the two Blueprints – soul's and this manifestation - reflect each other. Once in a while, a similar fracture is going on in everyone. In the event that there is a part in the Blueprints, this especially identifies with a detachment between the male and female parts of our being. Bind together the male/female energy inside us is the most significant advance to encountering unity.

If there is a part between the male/female perspectives, one portion of the Blueprint might be absent. So, the Monad is available, yet their Twin Flame is generally absent. By uniting the Blueprint back and making it entire, their Twin Flame comes in and the customer approaches working with their mirror-self. Note: F#

Coming up next depends on my own numbering system to incorporate the other major chakras that I work with. The numbers are not significant, where the chakras are and what they "do" is:

The Thirteenth Chakra: Divine Heart Space/Star Tetrahedron Heart Center: is arranged somewhere between the Throat and Heart Chakras, over the Thymus, this is the chakra of Co-Creative Divine Consciousness, the acknowledgment of the Divine inside, Unconditional Love and sympathy for self as well as other people. At the point when we stir this middle, wellbeing is conceivably an indispensable piece of our way. Life takes on importance and satisfaction and we experience the delight of Love, which pours forward from this chakra.

At the point when completely actuated this middle becomes one Unified Chakra. This is important despite the fact that abound together chakra enables you at that point to adjust your physical, emotional, mental and profound bodies, and to fit their energy. Working with the brought together chakra you bind together the five higher and the ten lower chakras into one so they all capacity as per the recurrence of unequivocal love-based energy coursing through this Divine-Heart focus.

The Thymus organ controls the resistant system and our pace of maturing. It is completely practical when the physical body (organs and organs) uses the thymus-administering engrave. The thymus normally gets littler as we age. By tapping the thymus daily, you keep it enacted. It is said that specific commencements additionally keep the thymus actuated and that you will quit maturing after the inception. Reiki is one such inception, especially after Level II.

At the point when Divine flow is more straightforward and ground-breaking, we may move reliably through life on top of the Intention of Spirit. At that point as male (musings) and female (feelings) are never again opposing, legitimate hormone parity will start to be set up. Shading: relies upon the spirit's motivation; Note: F#

The Fourteenth Chakra: Quantum-Holographic Gateway to the Divine is situated between the knees and is the place the universe links with the physical. The link resembles a roadway and links us to everybody and everything in the Universe. We regularly have improper connections with others through the Web and give our endowments and gifts away to shroud ourselves. Healing energy can be coordinated through the Web so as to fix the Web and in this way mend the "physical" body – which just seems strong yet is in certainty energy. If the physical body is harmed the Web is also harmed - torn or broken. Shading: Green-White Note: B

The Fifteenth Chakra: Physical Gateway to the Divine is between the feet, at the degree of the lower legs, and grounds and links the soul into the physical plane. At the point when this inside is initiated, we feel connected with Mother Earth and feel one with her energy, and that of all living things - alluded to by Native Americans as All My Relations. Natural consciousness lives here and our longing to help our Earth Mother. Shading: Navy Blue; Note A

The Sixteenth Chakra: Earth Star is roughly 18 inches beneath our feet and when initiated grounds our Spirit-Self completely into the physical into the Infinite Moment of the Present, where we are the most dominant - Spirit having a human encounter. We can't be something besides Spirit, in spite of the fact that people will, in general, overlook this Truth, and there is nothing to search for aside from inside oneself - to recollect that we are a bit of the Divine. Shading: Forest Green; Note A#

These 12 chakras, alongside other major and minor chakras, make up the most significant link between our soul and physical bodies. The chakras legitimately link with our sensory system, subsequently the significance of clearing the two systems - physical and energy bodies. At the point when we watch our examples (mentalities, values, and convictions), we consider pieces of information to be to what chakras are out of balance. There are many envisioning systems to bring the chakras into balance and arrangement and I would say they should be practiced each day.

CHAPTER THREE

Chakras Meditation

The Chakra Balancing Meditation

Chakra Meditation is subdivided into several circles, many eminently the Chakra adjusting manifestation as well as the Chakra fixing manifestation. The prior kind is intended for clearing and opening your mind, trapping and discharging any unwanted energies which are placed away within your system. It's similarly utilized to combine all of the greater recurrence energies. When doing Chakra Balancing manifestation, you ought to focus on all of the root chakras. When playing this out particular symptom, recollect what you ask what you may get.

The Chakra Healing Meditation

Chakra expression is similarly utilised to fix. The chakras which are triggered by Equal recuperating meditation is located in the lower spinal cord zone (on your coccyx bone) directly to the top of the head. These chakras include the Sacral Chakra, Root Chakra, Heart Chakra, Solar Plexus Chakra, Third Eye Chakra, Throat Chakra arguably the Crown Chakra. There are two strategies to take care of the Chakra regaining reflection. First, a meditator may focus on the motive level. This, you bring under account your current state and feelings. Can you truly feel rationally frustrated or bothered? Besides, an individual could focus on the consequences level. This meditation attempts to ease any consequences of branch and detachment instead of only observation these feelings.

Guided Chakra Meditation

Regardless if you are just beginning or you are experiencing trouble rehearsing chakra manifestation, a guided chakra meditation might just be exactly what you want. You are able to download a chakra meditation software using your mobile phone -- that there are such programs on the marketplace. You may also get support from several directed chakra meditation websites on the internet. Simply attachment on your earphones and tune into some chakra sensei because he compels you via altering methods.

Heart Chakra Meditation

The Forward chakra which structures the focus of the others is called the soul. This is where the psychological and physiological elements meet up. The centre chakra lies right in the focus of your torso. It contrasts to the centre as well regarding the thymus manhood, cardiovascular and lungs plexus. Heart chakra manifestation is intended for opening upward meditators' heart, permitting them to communicate pardoning, compassion, and love. People with closed or unequal heart palpitations will generally have unsavoury characters, as an instance, scorn, jealousy, outrage, and distress. The heart chakra manifestation is along these lines crucial for many chakra meditators.

What Is Chakra Meditation?

Reflection is a deep routine with respect to bitterness and mindfulness. It is not such a fantastic number about calming the mind as viewing, and away from it. The further grounded our capability to see the mind without reacting, the further we allow our internal mind, intuition, clairvoyant finds, and affiliation with spirit to stir.

There are various kinds of meditation. There's quiet reflection, in which one conveys their thought concerning the breath, or even regions of the human body and tenderly observe the musings. In guided discussions, we embark on an experience beyond the physical universe, in which art helps to focus on and tune in to soul and energy. Strolling expressions teaches you to take note of your surroundings – the landscapes, the aromas, the noises. Reciting meditation asks a mantra or even an official expression, that's repeated musically to reach a state of daze. Development meditation consolidates audio and proceeds to take focus on the realms of the human body as well as the frequencies of audio. Composing, drawing, creating, and much unremarkable errands, for example, collapsing clothes and cooking may similarly be forms of meditation. Numerous approaches work for a variety of people, the basic target would be to purify the justification, self-made left cerebrum and achieve deep stability and attention.

Chakra thought is a certain sort of meditation that aims blocked. With valid chakra manifestation, you are able to clean,

clean, and equalization to your mind. A vast assortment of practices comprises meditation. Some are committed to deep arousing; others into recuperating or relaxing. Psychological practice should be tried with an armed instructor.

Chakra reflection is perhaps among the most certainly one of a type plus also a point by point kind of meditation on the market --and it's also among the most satisfying. While frequently, the huge bulk jelqing chakra manifestation are further grown professionals--that is a sort of meditation which for all intents and purposes anyone can genius, whenever they understand the bolts and nuts.

Even though careful reflection is truly fundamental and can be connected with being in that time--chakra meditation originally needs an understanding of the identifying chakras or concentrates on energy that appear throughout your entire body. As these lines, even before it's possible to comprehend chakra reflection you need to understand the chakras, exactly what they mean and keeping them corrected is essential.

Chakra Meditation as a Way of Healing Mind, Body, and Spirit-Soul

Chakra Meditation is your way to physical health, ardent steadiness, and psychological clearness. That's about the grounds our chakras be conductors, dividing energy in the skies and ground with the aim they can contribute together. Chakras are really energy vortexes. The unification of the energies is what constructs a chakra. It's a vortex of transferring vitality, which in the point invigorates distinct endocrine organs within the human body to emit hormones into the flow system. Chakras are depicted as a type of pipe using littler pipes inside that station. They are also frequently contrasted with appearing like lotus blossoms. Numerous similarly have instinctively noticed the entrance of human chakras as appearing like the borders of a buff or even a windmill pivoting in around motion.

Chakras are entryways that encircle our prana-life power to flow throughout our air. Their focal point for existing is always vitalizing the body, also to promote arousing of our hesitation. They're connected with physical, psychological and emotional resources. There are seven important chakras that are all about sensed.

The air is often thought to be the eighth chakra. Our very first chakra (origin) actually reaches outside of their body. It's placed at the centre of your thighs… just someplace between the knees as well as your physical body. The seventh chakra, called the crown chakra, is organized on the maximum point of your mind. The rest of the chakras, (sacral, sunlight-oriented plexus, heart, neck, and eye), are cemented in series along the spine/neck, and skull. Independently, chakras seem like pipes using petal-like openings. Regardless of how chakras aren't clear to your eye, they are sometimes observed mystically via ready unpretentious vitality laborers.

The Significance of Chakra meditation

Having the chakras broke down and handled with a commendable and expert person ready in inconspicuous energy work is an extraordinary way of figuring out the way the body functions to an unnatural level. Magical vitality laborers which are ready in handling chakra meditation is going to have the choice to show to you that your chakras are in bad state, which ones have been drained, and what you can to burn off this burden. If, for example, the overtraining is doing on a lower degree, the rest of the movement will probably be forced to obtain a move on. Non-working chakras can "success" a normally audio type, which is definitely not terrific. By similarity, if individuals' hip or back renders arrangement, an individual will go to your chiropractor's office to get a change. In like fashion, an psychological energy labourer that's ready to control the energy flow can assist you in getting searing chakras balanced back into working state. It may expect a few sessions with a repairing specialist to acquire energy degrees back up to pace. From this stage, you may take a range of health actions to keep the chakras available and functioning ideally, which permits your energy to flow normally.

The Art of Chakra Meditation

With Such a substantial number of several types of meditation available, Chakra expression is frequently overlooked or overlooked. At the stage when you're picking a plan for you it's important that you put aside the attempt to determine precisely how this kind of manifestation can enhance your physical, enthused and deep health.

Be this as it might, akin to some substantial bunch of unique kinds of Chakra meditation, it's important that you see precisely what this kind of manifestation can reach for you. Compared to unique kinds of meditation, management of this Chakra centres from the body is able to straightforwardly correct how you feel. This is due to the manner this kind of meditation is recognized with all the vital parts of the human body. These seven important parts of the human body, also called Chakra centres, are called the Base, Sacral, Solar Plexus, Heart, Throat, Brow and Crown. In these groupings of concentrates will be the substantial organs such as the lungs, liver, cerebrum, heart and spine.

Before you can use Chakra manifestation, you need to put aside the attempt to determine precisely how these seven components of your Chakra will enhance your health. For example, focusing to the Solar Plexus stage may affect your psychological mood. The Solar Plexus (or yellowish chakra) is organized near the upper abdomen. With valid processes, you can affect your personal behaviour. It's possible to change a terrible mindset to an adequate person if you're careful with your strategy and management of the stage.

Wholeness is accomplished via a process of self-recognition, re-gathering along with re-association. Someone yields into direct participation together as a whole individual, alluded by a few as the "Higher Self," "Spirit," "Superconscious", "Greater Head," "I AM," or "Wholeness" that is only the institution whatsoever." "In this condition the oblivious and conscious are the individual may emanate energy completely from all of their targets of strength and consciousness, which comprises the 7 chakras. By emptying (evacuating/changing) energy blockages and discharging energy captured from the inconspicuous energy frame, a person feels, recoups and blatantly re-encounters older parts of self that were lost from the very first partition out of God. Within our voyage through life most have stockpiled dread, anguish, fear of distress, hatred, hurt and outrage. The Rapid Healing Method affects adverse emotions to adoration.

An In-Depth Guide to Your Properties and Functions of the 7 Chakras

Also, because there are just seven colours from the rainbow variety, seven levels of consciousness, seven phases of seven and man notes about the western scale, and you will find seven important moves within the body. You will find five chakras beyond the body which assist us in connecting with the prevalent field. The chakras are energy concentrates, transformers and entryways that port the meridian lines along with the three (3) qualities surrounding the bodily and bodies that are senile. They're located along the backbone and upwards to the mind and may be triggered and corrected together with the chakra manifestation churns from the conclusion of the report.

The First Chakra or root Chakra are discovered at the bottom of their spine, between your thighs. It is Sanskrit title is Muladhara and it's probable among the most important of all of the Chakras due to the soundness it provides us. This Chakra is the one which a lot of people suffer from and will need to have it adjusted together with the various Chakras.

This Origin Chakra is the own portrayal controller, of your capability to survive and of your overall wealth. It may earn a craving for relaxation and fiscal dependability, a longing for endurance and also to get a good association with the entire world.

Success and wealth issues may benefit from external assistance from the initiation of the Chakra as thoughts of comfort and fiscal security are often connected with an adequate origin Chakra.

If that the origin Chakra is not as available as it might be and continues to be turning slower than it's normal, then this may hinder nearly all the newly referenced perspectives and trigger difficulties on these lands. Some physiological side effects may similarly be calmed by using an obstructed root Chakra, one of these are reduced back problems, haemorrhoids, cardiovascular disease, flushing, awful dissemination along with weight reduction.

The Chief shading connected with this Chakra is reddish. Its alloy is iron and its own part is Earth. Its stones are crimson, hematite and red jasper. By using these stones, especially the red jasper, you are able to create a health forcefulness on your wellbeing and your own basic endurance troubles. Lethargic energy inside us may be stirred that will aid with interfacing more together with all the ground. Nearly all the lower Chakras could be rid of considering with this rock that could allow you to prove to be grounded. For bashful people or reluctant individuals this rock, when utilized to correct the origin Chakra can progress boldness and calibre.

At The stage in this Chakra is in equalization, the psychological angles provide you control over your own creative will along with your own confidence.

At The stage once the origin Chakra is outside from equalization be that as it might, childishness, discouragement and bashfulness are overriding with a tendency towards disturbance as well as an inadequacy to put aside money.

For Adapting this Chakra, you are able to use music for reflection that's at the key of C. Essentially envision a wad of crimson light round the lands of the origin Chakra.

The 7 chakras in your body feel the complete range of frequencies entering a Person's near home energy area. They process and disseminate energy entering the airs and meridians altering the frequencies to different Senses; to be particular, sense, thought and bodily senses. This is done similarly the eye refracts light. Also, as many frequencies of Light which enter the brain are obscured from the cerebrum as many colours, the seven Chakras, by refracting unpretentious energy, separate it to beliefs That emanate and influence on a person.

As transformers, the seven chakras are organs of transmutation. They measure up the energy or down because it passes from different energy sources to the discreet energy frame relying upon which system (physical, psychological or enthused) is at a lack position. That means you're able to say the transformers (chakras) equilibrium the energy as it passes the unpretentious energy frame. This is what occurs in recuperating. Abundance energy from the emotional and psychological bodies is transmuted into the body for strengthening itself.

Transmutation moves in four ways – down, up, inside, and outside. The seventh chakra within the body is an entryway which transmutes energy gleaned in the deep airplanes, which would be the most remarkable frequencies which enter somebody's energy area. Vitality in the physical body is able to be transmuted up to be used in the bigger bodies. Vitality from surrounding vitality fields could be transmuted because it moves through somebody's atmosphere and goes to a particular chakra that's touchy into its recurrence. A person may extend beams of energy out in their own heirs to somebody else's energy area, transmuting this up or down with respect to the vibration of their energy, frequently through explicit types of chakra manifestation.

CHAPTER FOUR

Understanding And Connecting With The Chakras

Connecting Your Chakra Power

There are various strategies we can use at home to help recuperate our chakras, including representations and meditations, changing old habits, rehearsing yoga, utilizing crystals and essential oils, and taking advantage of our nourishment. Since various individuals feel attracted to various healing processes, a scope of techniques is canvassed in this book. I, for the most part, prescribe that my patients pick healing systems that they feel most attracted to since one process isn't really superior to the next.

That being stated, in case you're encountering physical issues, it might start with dietary changes, yoga, back rub, acupuncture, and other bodywork first. If your fights identify with the brain or heart, meditation, gem work, or essential oils may be a decent beginning stage.

Meditation and Visualizations

Meditation is a type of mental exercise that prepares the mind to remain concentrated on a specific item, objective, or sensation, for example, your breath.

Reason

Meditation is an approach to quiet mental prattle. At the point when practiced normally, it can help change consciousness in a way that advances internal harmony, mental clearness, passionate energy, profound knowing, and focus, as well as ground us when we feel dissipated. By keeping up a particular center, similar to the breath, a mantra, or another apparatus, the brain can quit meandering and losing all sense of direction in thoughts, feelings, or other mental interruptions. Thoughts can also incorporate perceptions, where you make a psychological picture toward a particular reason. Imagining the hues or flow inside a chakra can assist you with associating with them and fortify them.

Since meditation includes the capacity to watch diverting thoughts and feelings without judgment, we figure out how to control our responses to improvements that may some way or another make difficult or upsetting responses. This ability—called care—can be an unimaginably useful asset for developing quiet and empathy in your everyday life. For the reasons for this book, it can also be a method for associating with, and reinforcing your chakras. You can utilize meditation to connect with what you're holding in a specific energy focus, helping you become progressively connected with your physical and energy bodies.

How It's Implemented

There are numerous approaches to contemplate—you can be sitting or resting, you can be still or think while taking part in a movement, for example, strolling, making craftsmanship, playing music, or journaling. A few people practice 5 to 10 minutes every day, while others may reflect for more. Later on in this book, we'll spread diverse meditation practices that help mend the distinctive chakras. Most won't expect you to reflect for longer than 5 to 10 minutes one after another.

Why/How It Works

Meditation is a training that has been tried and true all through the ages. It has delighted in a resurgence of enthusiasm for the recent years, no uncertainty despite even though most of us need to develop a training to calm our brain and make harmony inside our bustling ways of life! In any case, it's not only a craze.

Pros/Cons of Using This Method

Pros: On the positive side, meditation should be possible whenever, anyplace, inside whenever outline. It makes a more profound connection with oneself and makes it simpler for us to move into higher awareness. It also causes us get to our ability to self-mend and make care, which at that point expands harmony into the remainder of our lives. Also, in light of the fact that this training expands upon itself, meditation assists with any self-study practice you may already have.

Cons: Two words: "monkey mind." Your mind will need to occupy you from your training, regularly by calling up errands for the afternoon, similar to what you will have for supper, or thoughts you have been staying away from, such as stressing over your investment funds. Indeed, even prepared practitioners of meditation experience monkey mind. Meditation is known as a "practice" for an explanation: developing a feeling of profound mindfulness and inward harmony utilizing meditation requires some investment. It's anything but a medium-term handy solution.

Changing Old Habits

Getting out from old unfortunate habits can assist you with healing awkward nature in your chakras by making new, more advantageous habits.

Reason

Lifestyle and behavioral changes assist us with intruding on our normal regular examples of reasoning and responding to the earth. As a rule, unbalanced characteristics that we hold in our chakras can be recuperated, to some degree, by moving our awareness around long-standing convictions about ourselves and how we link with others.

How It's Implemented

The initial step to getting out from old habits is by being mindfulness of the negative behavior pattern, as well as making mindfulness around an issue that we are holding in a particular chakra. When we're mindful of an issue conduct or negative behavior pattern, we would then be able to work to change that conduct, or react in an unexpected way.

For instance, think about when you don't support yourself in a romantic relationship. Not communicating your needs and needs can be a sign that your throat chakra isn't adjusted. To interfere with this example, you may give careful thought at whatever point you see yourself closing down after a warmed discourse. When you're mindful you are hushing yourself, stop and ask how you could respond in an unexpected way. At that point, apply the new response. Any new response will meet this objective however profitable; sound responses will be more useful than unfortunate or rash ones. Maybe you link with your accomplice, such that they can hear you, about how the warmed discourse made you feel. Thusly, you help mend the hushing design in your throat chakra. We also change the account of recognizing as "somebody who keeps their mouth shut" to "somebody who is attempting to convey adequately."

Shifting awareness around an old pattern takes practice and persistence. In any case, doing it long enough enables us to get out from under old habits that never again serve us and make more beneficial ones.

Why/How It Works

This works on the grounds that by balancing our way to deal with a common issue, we are effectively drawn in with changing old examples that never again work.

At the point when rehearsed long enough, and with consistency, we clear old examples and convictions held in explicit chakras.

Pros/Cons of Using This Method

Pros: It works! Grasping new habits and utilizing them to supplant negative old habits brings positive, sound results, regardless of whether you still can't seem to completely link with your chakra system.

Cons: It can require some serious energy and a great deal of redundancy (and persistence) before the new examples stick.

YOGA

While there are numerous types of yoga, the one most ordinarily rehearsed spotlights on asana, the arrangement of physical stances and breathing activities planned for strengthening us physically, rationally, and profoundly.

Reason

Asana is the program of physical stances that give physical quality and stamina and are intended to make mindfulness and connection with the body through development. Asana yoga is an extraordinary device for self-change on different levels— physical, mental, and psychological.

How It's Implemented

Through physical activities and breath, we connect the mind with the tissues of our body. An assortment of yoga stances helps open different areas inside the body, which carries mindfulness and parity to the chakras. When rehearsing yoga asanas, we move the body into various physical stances and afterward hold those stances for set timeframes. Simultaneously, we control our taking in various ways, helping energy course all through the body and developing care. There are diverse yoga styles, some of which can be especially helpful in balancing the chakras. Kundalini yoga, for instance, utilizes explicit physical stances, reciting, breathing processes, and meditation to attempt to stir the Kundalini energy that travels through our chakras.

Further developed yoga stances have a higher danger of damage (headstand and shoulder remain, for instance, are not suitable for amateurs or anybody with neck damage) and ought to be finished with the help and direction of a prepared yoga instructor.

Why/How It Works

Yoga brings fundamental life power into the chakras, making mindfulness and opening the chakras. All in all, yoga helps with establishing us in our bodies through a tangible encounter. This is really helpful for those of us who will in general invest an excessive amount of time in our minds, occupied with mental exercises, and less time established in the Earth's energy, or completely present in our physical bodies. It additionally points out how our stances influence how we travel through the world.

For instance, when we experience melancholy, we tend to present our shoulders, making an inward development with our bodies. In connection to our energy body, we do this to ensure our heart chakra.

Nonetheless, if we keep this stance for quite a while, it can make physical issues in the shoulders or upper back. Rehearsing yoga causes us to become mindful of the snugness in our shoulders and upper back, draw in with it, and at last discharge it.

Pros/Cons of Using This Method

Pros: Because yoga requires a ton of physical development, it very well may be a magnificent type of activity. Yoga classes will in general be held in calm studios, so they can be relaxing and extraordinary for stress the executives. Since yoga develops familiarity with the body, a few people discover it encourages them practice more beneficial dietary patterns and other constructive way of life changes. Additionally, yoga doesn't for the most part require a great deal of costly hardware.

Cons: Yoga classes can be costly, and they may not fit into everybody's calendars. While there are many free yoga recordings web based, learning yoga as a novice can be troublesome on the grounds that without an instructor to manage them, it very well may be difficult to know whether one is rehearsing explicit stances appropriately. Some new experts experience pain, particularly migraines or muscle irritation, while their body acclimates to the stances, energy shifts, and physical effort of yoga practice. It additionally requires some investment to acquire ideal outcomes from yoga, and yoga must be done related to self-study and development of stillness to genuinely bolster chakra healing.

Crystals

Crystals are utilized to draw out or divert energy, as well as to build up the qualities related with a specific stone. They are additionally used to rebalance and recuperate.

Reason

Working with crystals and stones causes us to draw in with the characteristic Earth energy to sustain our qualities and blessings. It additionally encourages us to discharge what never again serves us, tap into our endowments, re-establish harmony, recuperate, and raise awareness. Crystals can be utilized from multiple points of view to address different difficulties.

How It's Implemented

There are numerous approaches to work with crystals. One basic route is to keep a little gem on your individual, regardless of whether worn as a pendant, studs, or arm jewelry or conveyed in your pocket. Conveying a gem on your body keeps its vivacious recurrence impacting you for the duration of the day. Another approach to work with stones, particularly when doing chakra healing, is to rests in an agreeable spot, place chakra-explicit crystals on their specific chakra, and enable yourself to ponder (or basically clear your brain) while the stones enhance what you're already taking a shot at— regardless of whether it be to discharge something from a certain chakra, develop your blessings, break examples, or work toward another objective. Another extraordinary method to utilize crystals is to hold them in your left (accepting) hand during meditation, so you can get the helpful healing vibrations of the gem.

Why/How It Works

Review our prior exchange of how everything is energy, vibrating at its own specific recurrence. Gems, as well, each have their own specific vibration and reason. By picking one to assist you with a specific objective, or by enabling yourself to be attracted to one specifically, you adjust yourself to the vibration of that stone, as it works legitimately with your energy body (and regularly benefits the physical body, too). For example, rose quartz helps the heart chakra, yet in addition, lessens pulse. It's everything related.

Pros/Cons of Using This Method

Pros: Crystals are stylishly satisfying to take a look at, viable, simple to utilize, and flexible to work with. The impacts of precious stone healing can also be effectively felt; you can actually feel the beating in your grasp when holding a gem that is ideal for what you're chipping away at.

Cons: It might set aside some effort to get comfortable with how to function with crystals. Cost and finding the correct crystals may also be testing—yet the Internet makes it simpler to locate the particular crystals you need at a decent worth.

Essential oils

Essential oil treatment is an antiquated healing practice that includes utilizing normal, regularly fragrant, exacerbates that exist in numerous sorts of plants for their healing properties.

Reason

Since finding the healing advantages of specific plants, herbs, and blooms, individuals discovered approaches to incorporate them in our lives—by adding them to suppers, making meditations with them, topically applying them to influenced regions, and refining their fragrance quintessence. While numerous individuals definitely realize that essential oils smell fragrant and charming, each plant additionally has its own emotional reverberation, enabling everyone to treat both the inconspicuous energy body and the physical body. For those of us who think excessively, fundamental oil treatment is incredible in light of the fact that it sidesteps our points of view and vibrates with us on a basic level. It can assist us with moving from being in a spot where feelings are overpowering, to a spot where we feel progressively ready to slowly inhale and slide into our subsequent stages. It is also valuable in bodywork, discharging strain in the muscles and treat explicit kinds of pain.

How It's Implemented

To help the chakras recuperate, applying 5 to 6 drops of a specific fundamental oil to a certain chakra can ground, focus, discharge, or open it. Blend a couple of drops of your chose basic oil in a transporter oil and apply the picked oils with a cotton ball, or back rub them into the chakra legitimately. When utilizing essential oils on the body, make certain to weaken them in bearer oils—especially those that are profoundly aggravating to the skin when utilized alone.

They're called bearer oils since they really convey the basic oil for application. A decent transporter oil to utilize is jojoba, which you can discover at your nearby wellbeing nourishment store. You can improve the healing experience by joining a thoughtful practice directly after utilization of the essential oils.

Why/How It Works

Essential oil uses go further than basically smelling pleasant. They get to our energy body and physical body, frequently interfacing them together in collaboration and making healing on different levels. They are especially powerful for chakra healing since they bring the energetics of the oil to the chakra, helping us link with it. Furthermore, even though healing occurs on a base level, it sidesteps the mind, promptly getting to our inner healing.

Pros/Cons of Using This Method

Pros: The healing that fundamental oil treatment brings is rapidly open. Quality oils are additionally simple to discover, they can go with you, and there are numerous approaches to work with them (by applying them to the body, diffusing them in your living or workspace, making mixes and elixirs, among others).

Cons: Because some essential oils may bother the skin, they are not suggested for topical application without a bearer oil. Additionally, ingesting oils isn't suggested, in light of the fact that they can excite the stomach related tract, and a few oils (contingent upon the maker) are contaminated. What's more, albeit basic oil treatment is amazing, it ought to be utilized related to different modalities to develop inward healing to assist you with accomplishing chakra balance.

Food and Diet

Food isn't just an approach to continue your physical body, however, an approach to help your energy body also—the food sources you eat can help your chakras recuperate vigorously.

Reason

With regards to chakra wellbeing, on the grounds that your energy body is legitimately connected with your physical body, what you ingest matters. Indeed, even our water admission can influence your wellbeing. Progressively conscious nourishment decisions can go far to healing your body and advancing higher vibration of your chakras.

How It's Implemented

 In a perfect world, the body capacities at its best when eating nourishments that help its systems. Nourishments can be incendiary: Dairy and gluten, for example, can be provocative to skin, processing, and joint wellbeing, and sugar is fiery to different body parts and systems.

Sugars can make a negative effect for a considerable lot of us in the event that they're a major part of a dietary plan. Then again, expelling exceptionally prepared fixings, for example, white flour and white sugar, from your eating regimen is a straightforward move that can improve your wellbeing from various perspectives. At the point when you eat all the more spotless nourishments—nourishments that are less prepared, all the more economically gathered, occasional, natural, privately sourced, and made with less added substances and all the more entire fixings—your physical body benefits. At the point when your physical body benefits, your energy body benefits too.

Why/How It Works

Eating clean foods bolsters your physical and energy body wellbeing. Making mindfulness around which nourishments work and don't work for your body helps all your body's systems; for example, by advancing cell development, bone development, muscle, organ, and organ wellbeing, and mental capacities. By expansion, this all advantages your energy body.

Pros/Cons of Using This Method

Pros: There are numerous decisions and choices to help your physical and energy bodies with nourishment, and when you actualize them, it tends to recuperate both your physical and energy bodies.

Cons: Eating well is a lot more difficult than one might expect. Spotless, natural, reasonably developed nourishment can be costly, and it very well may be enticing to buy advantageous inexpensive food as opposed to prepare sound nourishment at home.

Reiki, Acupuncture, and the Chakras

With regards to working with an expert to rebalance the chakras, there are a couple of various modalities to consider. Here, we'll spread Reiki and acupuncture. Reiki is an energy healing process in which a practitioner demonstration to channel boundless life power energy to a patient or customer to help their physical, emotional, mental, and psychological healing and development. The Reiki practitioner goes about as a conductor, utilizing a delicate situation of ("hands-on" or "hands-off") to help balance the chakras. Reiki ought to consistently be attempted with a guaranteed Reiki expert.

Acupuncture, another customary process, utilizes exact needle situation to lighten physical, mental, and emotional indications. While there is no official agreement around whether you can mend the chakras with acupuncture (some contend it's anything but an energy healing methodology), acupuncture moves chi, and there are acupuncture centers on chakras. In that light, acupuncture might be able to address chakra irregular characteristics. Once more, acupuncture should just be attempted with an authorized practitioner.

Keeping up Balance in Your Daily Life

As we begin to open up into the intensity of our chakras, it is imperative to keep up our raised vibration—positive energy—in everyday life. Why? Since when we are healing ourselves on different levels and clearing our chakras of denser energies, it is essential to keep our energy and space clear and ensured, as well as keep our vibration resounding at a higher recurrence. This keeps up chakra balance.

Consistently develop care and practice appreciation

By routinely developing care, we keep ourselves in the present. At the point when we ruminate and get discouraged, we frequently choose not to move on. At the point when we experience uneasiness, we are agonizing over what's to come. Remaining in the present enables us to show up completely for ourselves. Rehearsing thankfulness also lifts vibration.

Keep up your energy through movement. Regardless of whether it be yoga, qi gong, or other physical movement, it is imperative to routinely keep up clearness of mind, body, and soul.

Bless yourself with holy white sage. Sacrosanct white sage is an herb utilized by Native Americans for its incredible clearing properties. It clears negative energy from your body or living space. Clearing a living space or ourselves with holy white sage is called smearing. To smirch a living space, light the tip of a lot of sage with a match or lighter; enable the smoke to crest; and utilize your hand or a quill wand to float the smoke to regions of the home, beginning clockwise from the front entryway, blessing all things along the way, until you arrive at the front entryway again. To smear yourself, utilize your hands to coordinate the smoke toward your body, blessing all pieces of your body, particularly your chakras down your midline. As you do as such, state resoundingly, "I bless my throat chakra, I bless my arms, I bless my chest, etc. Try to tap the free remains into a warmth safe holder sometimes as you come.

Epsom salt showers. Emotionally sensitive individuals—the individuals who get other individuals' energy effectively—ought to consider cleaning up once per week or each other week. Similar remains constant for the individuals who have physical a throbbing painfulness, particularly solid ones. Epsom salt contains magnesium, which is effectively absorbed through the skin during a shower and mitigates solid and other physical pain, as well as oversee pressure. What's more, it helps clear airs, which is particularly valuable for the individuals who will, in general, take work home, have a troublesome drive, work in a poisonous office, or manage troublesome individuals. Epsom salt showers are very detoxifying for your system and can even be utilized to avert colds.

Your Sacred Healing Space

To make a consecrated healing space, make a special stepped area at home. Some prescribed things incorporate the accompanying:

Sacred white sage pack. As referenced here, sacrosanct white sage is utilized to smear yourself and an area. To smirch a living space, light the tip with a match or lighter, enable the smoke to tuft, at that point float the smoke to territories of the space to be smeared.

62

Palo Santo. Palo Santo, or "heavenly wood" in Spanish, originates from a tree that develops in Central and South America. It clears energy and unequivocally dispels antagonism, particularly wickedness spirits. Use it much equivalent to sacrosanct white sage.

Feather wand. Regardless of whether it is an enormous single quill or a wand heap of plumes, to smirch, utilize the quill wand to direct smoke toward territories to be purified.

Heat-resistant container. Utilize this to assemble the remains that may tumble from consuming sacrosanct white sage or Palo Santo.

Crystal allies. Keep extraordinary crystals to bless the altar space and raise the vibration of your raised area.

Photographs of precursors and friends and family. Keeping photographs of friends and family who have passed respects their memory, keeps the energy of their affection close, and, in the event that they are precursors, conjures their security and intelligence.

Candles. Light candles when respecting a progenitor, summoning connection with the Divine/Source/Universe/God/dess, or to enact the special raised area's energy.

Statues of divinities that have significance for you. A few people place statues that hold strict significance on their special raised area; others may have statues of gods they work intimately with.

A bowl for offering. This can be a bowl or other compartment that holds an organic product offering, water offering, or bloom advertising.

To continue living quarters without a worry in the world of negative or stale energies, it's also perfect to keep a spotless home. Do standard physical cleanings and downplay mess, since earth and residue also hold dormant energy.

At the workplace, putting a couple of crystals by the PC, workstation, or cell phones can help make a progressively adjusted workspace. Particularly helpful is dark tourmaline, since it squares and ingests electromagnetic contamination that PCs and different gadgets may radiate.

More so, setting up a working environment precious stone system is an incredible method to set up a defensive field among ourselves and those we work with, particularly if the workplace is dangerous. Taking four every one of dark tourmaline, clear quartz, or selenite and placing each piece into the four corners of a working environment (or home, or even your bedframe) makes this impact.

In the following area, we'll spread different physical, emotional, mental, and deep afflictions, side effects, and encounters that show up in our bodies when our chakras are uneven and study each chakra's healing processes in detail.

CHAPTER FIVE

Chakras Ailments And How To Identify Blocked Chakras

The reason for your fixing work would be to release everything that keeps your individual self from fully understanding that. Contingent on the chakras being invigorated, the indications and signs of the releasing or "preparing" change.

ROOT - 1ST CHAKRA

At the stage when this really is invigorated and opens upward, you might feel heat or exceptional warmth in a variety of portions of the entire body, especially at the bottom of the spine. Your body might feel overwhelming and invisibly to the ground, and you might start to put on fat reduction. Your toes may prove to be fragile, and you might feel spiralling (vortex) tails moving around. Your bodily association with character, the entire world, sustaining and developing matters (and people) proves to be important.

ASTRAL - 2ND CHAKRA

At the stage when this really is invigorated and opens, you might have a vast assortment of sensual meditations and thoughts. Over several lifetimes, you've had several close relationships with many spirits. On the off possibility there are really no stifled and insatiable sexual energies and relations of any of these, this can make itself understood, or will soon be dealt with astrally on your dreams (which aides helpfully interrupts the ponderousness of ethnic restrictions). At the stage once the energies (and karmas) of those institutions are ended, these links can become a progressively unrestricted kind of adoration, or else they will surely discharge and drop away.

Sun Powered PLEXUS - 3RD CHAKRA

At the stage in this really is invigorated and opens, anxieties may be discharged as body replacements, or as an extricating of their bowels (looseness of the bowels). At the stage when outrage has been discharged, then you might choose to shout and crying, and suddenly feel ill and hurl. You might stretch an all of the prominent nearness you did not have as the words have been permeated with force and power.

HEART - 4TH CHAKRA

At the stage when this really is revived and opens upward, you might believe it hurt or laborious - that shows that the heart is undergoing "developing pains," extending into the way it can cherish. At this time when distress is being discharged, then you might shout or yell abundantly within the tiniest matters, or even so for reasons unknown by any stretch of your imagination. The centre is a very delicate attention - it seems that which profoundly. You might have periods in which you love everybody. Also, what's beautiful and perfect.

THROAT - 5TH CHAKRA

At the stage when this really is revived and opens, you might choose to speak bountifully and quickly, or singing suddenly and emotionally. You will hear inner noises, melodies, voices or clamour. Your clairvoyance opens and you're able to discover people's shrouded musings along with expectations. Expressions and words start to possess more energy and significance, and you are able to sense the vibrations of people just by their own words.

Forehead - 6TH CHAKRA

At the stage when this particular spectacle - otherwise referred to as the "next Eye" - is invigorated and opens upward, you might have a shivering electric feeling in your brow (or just sense a burden). You will observe colours, shadows, images, luminous lights, atmospheres or spirits (along with phantoms). Previous presence situations may occur inside your inner eyesight, along with your dreams may become clear and seem to be somewhat real.

CROWN - 7TH CHAKRA

At the stage when this really is invigorated and opens upward, you might feel as though your mind is being worked - such as someone is remaining needles or sticks on the skull (or hauling out them). You might have headaches cerebral distress - signals that energy squares have been dealt with. At the stage when stuck energies have been discharged, you might have shivering senses and also heat on your body (especially on your back, head, feet, and hands). There could shoot feelings of electricity traveling through your spinal column, also blasts along with blasts of lights. Instincts can come efficiently without deduction - that you just comprehend what is "real."

More Symptoms and Ailments

Addiction

The affected chakras - generally the throat chakra, however, all different chakras are affected

Addition happens when we become reliant on a legitimate or illicit medication, substance, nourishment, or conduct. Long-standing addition can cause significant issues for us seeing someone, our physical, mental, and psychological wellbeing, our work, and with the legitimate system. At the point when we are experiencing compulsion, we have lost correspondence with ourselves as well as other people, feel quieted, and feel incapable to communicate. These are on the whole qualities that include an out-of-balance throat chakra.

In spite of the fact that addition is for the most part identified with the throat chakra, different chakras may make the dependence happen or proceed. At the point when we feel embarrassed about what our identity is, or self-cure to abstain from handling difficult feelings, our sacral plexus chakra is included. In the event that feelings of low self-esteem or feebleness have had a major impact in the compulsion, our sun-oriented plexus chakra is included. If we are in our dependence because of not feeling grounded, or feel like we should do it to endure, our root chakra might be shouting out for help. If it is an endeavor to calm our wrecked heart, or we feel disengaged from ourselves, our heart chakra is at the foundation of our concentration. Our crown chakra is engaged with addition when we feel separated from the Divine and feel alone on the planet.

Therefore, the third eye chakra's capacity to see more than what is in our physical viewable pathway, (for example, having mystic capacities or believing what we don't yet have the foggiest idea or comprehend) can be a piece of an individual's addition; the addictive conduct might be a push to numb these clairvoyant capacities, in light of the fact that an individual may discover them terrifying or not get them.

Adrenal Fatigue

The *affected chakra- root chakra, sacral plexus chakra*

Adrenal fatigue happens when we are presented to constant stress. Our adrenal organs become burdened by the consistent elevated pressure reaction, rendering adrenal wellbeing deficient. Under typical conditions, the adrenal organs trigger the arrival of cortisol (also called the pressure hormone), which steps in to assist us with taking care of pressure. Adrenaline, our fight-or-flight hormone, is additionally placed moving by our adrenals. Both of these hormones are enacted to assist us with escaping distressing circumstances.

This is incredible when utilized on a transient premise. In any case, those experiencing adrenal exhaustion have been running on vacant because of a ceaseless pressure reaction. A few indications of adrenal fatigue incorporate general tiredness, body hurts, unexplained weight reduction, low pulse, unsteadiness, loss of body hair, and skin staining (hyperpigmentation). Since the adrenals are the organs of the root chakra and the sacral plexus chakra, any issues around adrenal weariness, including tending to the cause(s) of stress themselves, ought to be investigated. Since the root chakra manages issues around having a sense of safety, grounded, and stable, it merits investigating zones of unbalance in our lives. It's additionally worth investigating issues around power and confidence, which are qualities identified with the sacral plexus chakra.

Anger

The affected chakra - for the most part root chakra; however, different chakras are influenced

Anger, without anyone else, is a solid feeling. It causes us go to bat for ourselves, make solid limits, start activity and change, and break unsafe circumstances. In any case, when it is unexpressed, directed in unfortunate ways, or damages ourselves or others, it can cause conflict in our lives.

At the point when we are irate over a circumstance or at somebody, the root is regularly fear—fear that our wellbeing, business, or endurance is being compromised. Along these lines, anger frequently resounds with the root chakra, which is our endurance chakra.

However, fear transforming into anger can influence the different chakras, as well. For example, our crown chakra may need balancing in the event that we have an inclination that we've been managed a terrible turn throughout everyday life and resent the Divine/Source/Universe/God/dess for the apparent shamefulness. Our third eye chakra might be included if we are not in contact with our emotional insight, we can't trust past what we can physically observe, (for example, being disappointed with a present circumstance without seeing the pro plan, nor believing that we have alternatives other than what's before us), and we depend just on our mind. If we feel activated into anger by being hushed or unfit to convey what needs be, our throat chakra is out of agreement. If our anger is because of feeling like our heart has been stomped all over, we're centered on past damages, we feel forlorn, or we think that it's difficult to excuse, our heart chakra needs healing. In the event that we are furious on the grounds that we have been put in an undesirable power dynamic (like managing dangerous colleagues or an unfortunate relationship), or if we feel things are wild in our lives, our sun-based plexus chakra is out of balance.

Finally, our sacral plexus chakra may be out of parity if our imagination is being smothered or our feelings are quelled. Our anger can be stewing and may in the end explode, out of the blue. Our displeasure will also originate from here when we have encountered sexual maltreatment or feel our sexuality has been compromised.

Anorexia and Bulimia

The affected chakra - solar plexus chakra

Anorexia is a dietary problem described by strangely low body weight, a contorted view of one's weight, and serious fear of putting on weight. People experiencing anorexia seriously confine the measure of nourishment they eat. Bulimia, then again, is the point at which an individual gorge (or eats a lot of nourishment), trailed by a scene of cleansing—frequently through constrained spewing, taking purgatives, or doing undesirable degrees of activity. Since both dietary issues are about brutally making a decision about one's physical appearance, likening slenderness with self-esteem, and attempting to control one's own mental self-worth to address apparent physical blemishes, anorexia and bulimia both outcome in an out-of-balance sun-oriented plexus chakra, the power revolve for issues around control, confidence, and certainty.

Anxiety

The affected chakras - all chakras, contingent upon what kind of anxiety

Incidental anxiety is frequently a piece of ordinary everyday life. However, when a feeling of exceptional, extreme, and tireless stress saturates our regular presence, it very well may be crippling. For some who experience the ill effects of tension, it can top into fear or fear inside minutes, causing a fit of anxiety. In many cases, it can meddle with our personal satisfaction.

Contingent upon what sort of uneasiness you may have, any of the chakras might be included. For example, the crown chakra being out of balance may cause uneasiness if we feel like the Divine/Source/Universe/God/dess doesn't have our back. If our anxiety is brought about by an imbalance in the third eye chakra, it is typically on the grounds that we don't confide in our very own instinct and feel on edge about the obscure. If it is brought about by a throat chakra that is out of agreement, we are restless about conveying everything that needs to be conveyed, speaking with others, and saying how we truly feel. In the event that we are clutching past damages, or, then again, if we are on edge since we are separated from our feelings, our heart chakra might be out of parity.

In the event that we feel on edge since we are just overpowered by everything, feel scared, feel trapped in some sort of intensity dynamic in a relationship, or feel strain to perform well in our lives, our out-cockeyed solar plexus chakra is causing our tension. In the event that our sacral plexus chakra is included, blame or disgrace is moving our uneasiness, generally over extreme feelings that haven't been completely prepared. This also happens when there's tension identified with past injury, particularly sexual injury. If we are feeling restless about our material endurance in this world (nourishment, haven, cash, etc), our root chakra is out of parity, making us feel like we are in steady endurance mode.

Asthma and Allergies

The affected chakras - heart chakra

At the point when we experience narrowing aviation routes, and they produce extra mucous, it can trigger hacking, wheezing, and brevity of breath. At the point when we have hypersensitivities, our safe system makes antibodies that distinguish a particular allergen as unsafe, regardless of whether it may not be. The two conditions can influence one's personal satisfaction. As a rule, these conditions are because of an undermined invulnerable system and may cause respiratory trouble and irritation in our skin, aviation route, sinuses, or stomach related system. However, on the grounds that they are in the domain of the heart chakra, some of the time these sorts of physical responses can be connected to an imbalance in that chakra, especially if we are having issues around melancholy, despair, love, and empathy.

Back Pain

Pain in any territory of the back—upper back, center back, or lower back—that hasn't been brought about by physical injury or dull physical pressure might be saying something regarding chakra wellbeing. Pain can go from a dull incessant throb that keeps the back tight to sharp intense pain that breaking points scope of movement.

Upper Back

The affected chakras - throat chakra, heart chakra

Some of the time, when we are not talking our fact or when we are encountering awfulness, a danger to self-esteem, or trouble in adoration with others, the subsequent pressure can really show physically as strain or pain in the upper back. We may also be feeling unsupported, disliked, or that we are keeping down adoration.

Middle Back

The affected chakras - heart chakra, solar plexus chakra

At the point when we have issues around affection, feeling adored, clutching past damages, or feeling tested in our capacity, we may encounter strain or pain in the middle back. Some of the time this happens on the grounds that we are stuck in those past feelings, and may feel racked with a feeling of blame over what we have done or said to make a circumstance.

Lower Back

The affected chakras - sacral plexus chakra, root chakra

At the point when we are feeling tested in our wealth, connections, and innovative articulation; keeping down feelings or essentially not preparing them; having issues around endurance and acquiring the fundamental necessities, we may endure pressure and pain in the lower back. We may particularly have back pain (not because of physical injury) when we feel monetarily unsupported.

Cancer

The affected chakras - all

Cancer happens when strange cells create and partition wildly, invading and annihilating ordinary body tissue. It can occur on a wide range of levels, and the side effects change contingent upon which parts of the body are influenced. A few side effects incorporate exhaustion, weight changes, skin changes, substantial bumps or territories of thickening under the skin, unexplained and industrious muscle or joint pain, and unexplained and tenacious fevers or night sweats, among others. Components known to build danger of malignancy incorporate age, habits, family ancestry, wellbeing conditions, and condition. However, the Mayo Practice expresses that most of cancers happen in individuals who don't have any realized hazard factors whatsoever. As far as energy, malignant growth can be the aftereffect of long-standing disdain and profound hurt that has been left natural, disregarded, or denied, showing in conveying contempt, anguish, or other poisonous feeling that destroys oneself.

These can show on numerous levels, and because of irregularity in different chakras:

Lung cancer: Throat and heart chakras

Cancers of thyroid, larynx, and throat: Throat chakra

Brain tumours: Crown chakra

Cancers of stomach, liver, digestion tracts, and pancreas: Solar plexus chakra

Breast cancer: Heart chakra

Prostate and rectal cancer: Sacral plexus and root chakras

Cancers of cervix, ovaries, uterus, colon, and rectum: chakra

Codependency

The affected chakras - root chakra, heart chakra, solar plexus chakra, sacral plexus chakra

78

At the point when we are in a broken, uneven relationship — where we depend on our accomplice too much for the vast majority of our passionate and mental needs — we are said to be mutually dependent. Codependency also portrays a relationship that empowers someone else's unreliable conduct or addition, where one accomplice normally forfeits their needs and needs to help the other, to the point of surrendering portions of themselves, having poor limits and low confidence, feeling uncertain, and inadequately imparting excruciating feelings. Since mutually dependent connections are frequently founded on the fear of surrender and dismissal, there is an immediate connect to the root chakra, where fear-based activities and emotions originate from.

Codependency regularly emerges from youth, when a useless family overlooks or denies pain, fear, anger, or disgrace. This can incorporate when a relative is managing addition; when there is physical, emotional, or sexual maltreatment; or if a relative is experiencing a constant mental or physical sickness. Issues coming from uncertain family pain are additionally identified with the root chakra.

With codependency, there is additionally an unevenness in the heart chakra, fundamentally in light of the fact that we are centered on our adoration toward others instead of our affection for ourselves, which is frequently saved. It's a kind of separate from our heart focus. At the point when this chakra is out of balance, it can also prompt an absence of acumen seeing someone.

Since our confidence is tested because of, and after entering, a mutually dependent relationship, our solar plexus chakra is also influenced. If our sacral plexus chakra is unbalanced, at that point any feelings with respect to disgrace, blame, anger, and disdain will surface in a mutually dependent relationship, as well as an absence of sound limits.

Conflict

The affected chakras- throat chakra, at times solar plexus chakra and sacral plexus chakra

At the point when we are in strife with a person or thing, and we can't help contradicting what's going on or what somebody is letting us know, there is a difference in what is being communicated. At whatever point we have an issue around articulation and correspondence, the throat chakra is included.

Once in a while, we may stay away from strife inside and out, which is a variant of quieting ourselves. At the point when we quietness ourselves, we become angry, and the uncommunicated feelings stay repressed inside until we at last detonate. Regardless of whether we look for conflict, keep away from it, or basically end up inside it, our throat chakra is attempting to be heard. We are attempting to be heard, convey what needs be, and impart what we truly feel.

Conflict may also be an indication that our solar plexus chakra needs thought since strife can show that our own capacity is being tested, or that our sacral plexus chakra is included since the sacral plexus chakra is the seat of our feelings.

Constipation

The affected chakras - root chakra, potentially solar plexus chakra

Troublesome or rare solid discharges may demonstrate stoppage. Since the rectum and butt are at the degree of the root chakra, any dysfunctions including these pieces of our bodies can demonstrate that our root chakra is out of balance. It might be useful to think about whether you are feeling activated with endurance gives that are causing pressure—base needs like having nourishment to eat, water to drink, garments to wear, a home to stay in bed, and having a sense of security and secure. Since constipation is physically an aftereffect of an imbalanced stomach related system, it would also be useful to ensure the solar plexus chakra is adjusted. Encounters of fear, absence of certainty, absence of sense of pride, and trouble feeling in contact with our capacity may also influence the stomach related process, making colon or intestinal issues and different issues. Therefore, awkwardness in the solar plexus chakra may add to a root chakra's obstruction issue.

Depression

The affected chakras - crown chakra, heart chakra

Depression can occur for various reasons. Here and there it goes through briefly. Different times, it very well may be a consistent nearness in our lives. In many cases, for the individuals who experience the ill effects of ceaseless misery, it tends to incapacitate. Sorrow can feel like tenacious bitterness, vacancy, or sadness, the nonattendance of joy in everyday exercises, and as if life on occasion does not merit living. It can also influence our hunger and our rest—either keeping us up, or making us need a lot of rest.

In some cases, there will even be repetitive thoughts about death or suicide. At the point when we are discouraged, one of the primary main drivers is a profound inclination of forlornness. This is the reason sadness is principally connected to the crown chakra. At the point when we feel connected with the remainder of the world, and the Divine, our crown chakra is open and adjusted. At the point when we feel detached from the world, and even have anger toward the Divine at how our life has unfurled, it is normally a sign that our energy in this chakra is out of amicability. What's more, an unbalanced heart chakra may cause sorrow, because of the absence of connection with ourselves.

Digestive Issues

The affected chakras - solar plexus chakra

At the point when we experience issues processing issues that emerge in our real lives, we feel it vivaciously, as well. In the event that you've at any point lost your hunger, or on the other hand, had a covetous one as a reaction to push or overpowering news, you already comprehend the impacts of the solar plexus chakra.

Since this chakra is our capacity focus, when we feel tested in our capacity, for example, feeling low confidence, terrorizing, or frailty—this chakra gets imbalanced. What's more, along these lines, stomach related problems can result.

Detachment from Self and Others

The affected chakras - heart chakra

At the point when we are detached from what our identity is, from how we feel, and from our fantasies, interests, and what lights us up, our heart chakra is out of parity. Frequently, this first shows as disappointment with not feeling connected with others. We may end up investing significant stretches of energy independent from anyone else, yet not in a way that restores our soul or causes us feel connected with ourselves. It's typically to have with a general feeling of discomfort or discontent about existence. We need to feel cheerful, however don't, or are not in contact with what satisfies us. Here and there, we might be discouraged, which regularly happens when we are detached from ourselves. We all need to link— with ourselves and with others. It is designed into our human presence.

Individuals who are completely detached from themselves may not know that they are. They might be completely settled in their daily plan, living on autopilot or in endurance mode, not from a position of appreciation, commitment with what their identity is, or connection and attention to how their daily exercises make them feel. The individuals who can make mindfulness around their daily exercises, and even do brisk registration with themselves during the day, are progressively ready to make a connection with themselves, and can start a more beneficial connection with the heart chakra.

Fatigue

The affected chakras - solar plexus chakra, crown chakra

At the point when fatigue is continuous, increasing, or isn't diminished by rest, there is a consistent condition of exhaustion, and our energy stores feel drained. This influences concentration, center, energy, and inspiration, which inevitably impacts us vivaciously. If we are the sort who's inclined to adrenal fatigue, dependent on being occupied, or routinely exhaust ourselves, we are driving ourselves into weariness because of solar plexus chakra imbalance.

Exhaustion is identified with the solar plexus chakra, our capacity focus. At the point when we connect our confidence and self-assurance to our presentation in the working environment or throughout everyday life, we think about it literally if a task fizzles or has all the earmarks of being below average. We at that point work ourselves into a craze to meet a view of flawlessness, which results in weariness. Then again, if our exhaustion is because of sadness or feeling detached from the Divine, the crown chakra needs balancing.

Fear

The affected chakras - root chakra, solar plexus chakra

At the point when we feel fear, we see a person or thing as hazardous—we feel it will cause us hurt or is compromising our reality. Fear causes an adjustment in mind and organ work, enacting a course inside our thoughtful sensory system that brings us into fight or-flight mode.

It is a versatile conduct that encourages us recognize dangers and endure predators and catastrophic events. Fear is useful for endurance. However, being in this state for a really long time can contrarily affect our lives. A few gives that can trigger this base response are around essential endurance needs and having a sense of safety in our lives, neighborhoods, and families.

Whenever our essential needs are undermined, it makes an imbalance in the root chakra. Furthermore, in the event that we've been educated at an early age to remain in this fear, it can make long-standing root chakra disharmonies that influence us as grown-ups. Remaining in fear for significant stretches of time can also influence our hormonal system and cause adrenal fatigue. Another chakra that can be influenced when we feel fear is our solar plexus chakra. This is frequently an aftereffect of the underlying root chakra awkwardness. Not feeling bolstered in our fundamental needs can make a feeling of fatigue and challenge our confidence, the two of which are identified with the solar plexus chakra.

Despondency

CHAKRA AFFECTED heart chakra

It is beneficial to lament when we lose a person or thing valuable. Nonetheless, if the anguish is left natural, if we deny that it exists, or if we clutch it past its value in an unfortunate way, it can cause a square in the heart chakra. Whenever left unchecked, the awkwardness brought about by gripping melancholy for a really long time will make us feel forlorn, lose trust, or develop harshness. While lamenting, there might be a propensity to detach ourselves.

This, as well, can fill a need, since a few of us need the personal time to decompress and process how we're feeling. Nonetheless, in light of the fact that our heart chakra interfaces us to our self-esteem and love for other people, if we seclude ourselves for a really long time, our heart chakra experiences absence of connection.

We have to recall to reconnect, with ourselves, however with other individuals. Despite the fact that it might feel perpetual, everything changes and changes, including our discernment that we are always destroyed from those we love.

Blame

CHAKRAS AFFECTED sacral plexus chakra, solar plexus chakra

Blame is the inclination of having accomplished something incorrectly, regardless of whether the recognition is valid or not. This feeling is frequently identified with the sacral plexus chakra, which is the seat of our feelings. This energy focus is additionally connected with joy and the feelings of our sexuality. If we were educated to curb our sexuality or potentially feelings growing up, we regularly feel blame and disgrace in our grown-up life. Blame is intended to assist us with holding things under wraps. However, for the most part, this is an inefficient feeling that squares us from getting delight, and sound joy is the thing that we experience when our sacral plexus chakra is adjusted. Since blame can affect our confidence and our feeling of intensity, our solar plexus chakra can also be influenced. A major part of healing this, other than the sacral plexus and solar plexus chakra cures recorded in this book, is to enable ourselves to feel our feelings, as opposed to deny them or drive them down.

Migraine

CHAKRAS AFFECTED third eye chakra, crown chakra

At the point when we get migraines that aren't legitimately brought about by physical irregular characteristics, it very well may be a sign that there is disharmony in one of our chakras. At the point when you have frontal cerebral pains, with side effects, for example, sinus weight and weight behind your eyes that can spread to your temple, it is frequently a third eye chakra disharmony.

This sort of cerebral pain may demonstrate that we are concentrating just on our insight, fearing the psychological parts of ourselves, just ready to see the physical reality throughout everyday life and not confiding in our instinct. Once in a while, when these cerebral pains happen, it is on the grounds that we are disregarding the internal knowledge we have. At the point when we get natural "indications" yet don't follow up on them, we are not regarding our third eye intelligence. For instance, maybe you believe you should seek after another chance, however don't. Or on the other hand you experience a natural realizing that someone in particular may not be beneficial to cooperate with, however you go into a connection with them at any rate. Acting contrary to natural indications can cause conflict and a imbalance with your third eye chakra.

If you have a vertex cerebral pain (one that is at the top focus of the head), it might be brought about by an imbalanced crown chakra. This may show trouble confiding throughout everyday life or our way, seeing the bigger example or picture, or developing confidence in ourselves and our connection with the Divine. We may also feel alone or unsatisfied with life.

Hemorrhoids

CHAKRA AFFECTED root chakra

Hemorrhoids, also called heaps, are swollen veins in the butt and lower rectum. They might be found under the skin around the rear-end (outer hemorrhoids), or inside the rectum (inward hemorrhoids), and are like varicose veins. If they're not brought about by stressing during solid discharges, expanded weight on the veins during pregnancy, or one of numerous other physical causes, they might be brought about by a chakra irregularity.

Since the lower rectum and butt are at the degree of the root chakra, any brokenness that includes these pieces of our bodies can show that our root chakra is out of balance. This chakra is about endurance, so base needs like having nourishment to eat, water to drink, garments to wear, a rooftop over our heads, and having a sense of security and secure in our lives may emerge.

Hemorrhoids may also be emotionally connected to a fear of giving up, anger of the past, or feeling troubled.

Hip Pain

CHAKRA AFFECTED sacral plexus chakra

At the point when we experience issues in the hips, (for example, snugness, pressure, muscle fits, or pain), that aren't the consequence of physical injury to the zone or over working out, there is frequently a relationship to sacral plexus chakra issues.

Frequently, the hips can hold a ton of unexpressed feelings, as a rule feelings that haven't been managed, or that we've been keeping away from. Since the sacral plexus chakra is the seat of our feelings, we cause a imbalance here when we don't respect our emotions around a circumstance. Also, if we are feeling issues around communicating sound sexuality, especially around disgrace identified with our sexuality (another marker for a sacral plexus chakra unevenness), this can also cause snugness or pain in the hips.

Fruitlessness

CHAKRAS AFFECTED sacral plexus chakra, root chakra, solar plexus chakra

At the point when a lady can't imagine in spite of successive endeavors for at any rate a year, this is viewed as barrenness. Albeit many experience barrenness, the dissatisfaction and fear that ladies attempting to consider experience makes a lot of pressure, at times even disgrace. The sacral plexus chakra is included here, not just on the grounds that it is related with the belly and privates, yet additionally in light of the fact that it is the seat of our feelings. Numerous individuals who are managing barrenness fight through serious feelings, making them wonder: "Is this the correct choice?" "Would I even like to be a parent?" "Am I with the correct accomplice?" "Imagine a scenario where I'm not a decent parent?" and "In what manner will this completely change me.

Now and again, a physical reason or causes, for example, poor egg quality, low sperm check, absence of feminine cycle, high follicle-invigorating hormone (FSH), or different issues — are to be faulted. In any case, numerous different occasions, there is the segment of high weight with respect to the individuals attempting to imagine.

Since barrenness can trigger issues around family, the root chakra is also included. Other pull chakra thoughts for individuals attempting to consider emerge if they are attempting to construct a family when they're not getting support from critical relatives, or if they're worried about passing on bothersome family characteristics to their posterity. Also, in light of the fact that making another life can challenge one's confidence, frequently making them feel weak over their bodies, solar plexus chakra issues can result too, on the grounds that this energy focus is our capacity focus.

Jaw Pain/Temporomandibular Joint (TMJ) Pain

CHAKRA AFFECTED throat chakra

The temporomandibular joint (TMJ) interfaces your jawbone to your skull, and acts like a sliding pivot to open and close the mouth. We have one joint on each side of our jaw. Some of the time pain in the region can result from jaw damage, joint pain, hereditary qualities, or teeth grasping and pounding. Teeth pounding, or bruxism, can regularly be because of stress that is held in the jaw. It can also happen when we're attempting to keep down what we truly need to state or feel hushed, which is identified with our throat chakra.

Acupuncture, rubbing the masseter muscle (the muscle in your jaw that controls biting), and wearing a mouthguard around evening time can be useful for the physical parts of TMJ pain. TMJ pain may also be established in a lively part—feeling like we're not ready to support ourselves, state what we mean, or impart viably. TMJ pain can also result when we're feeling angry. To address the full picture of jaw help with discomfort, we not just need to inspect hotspots for physical alleviation, yet comprehend the possible vivacious causes too. If you end up keeping quiet when you truly need to state something, or you're gripping your jaw firmly to keep yourself down, it might be beneficial to look at what you are holding in your throat chakra, and why you are thinking that it's hard to state what's at the forefront of your thoughts.

Leg Pain

CHAKRAS AFFECTED root chakra, solar plexus chakra

Leg pain, when not straightforwardly identified with physical injury, is regularly connected to a root chakra imbalance. In some cases, leg pain can symbolize our opposition toward pushing ahead throughout everyday life, which can show as self-attacking practices dependent on fear—fear that we'll come up short, or fear that we'll really get what we need and venture into our capacity. If so, the root chakra irregularity can also be connected to the sun-oriented plexus chakra. In any case, it's for the most part a root chakra issue if the protection from pushing ahead is because of fear around bills, or picking up or losing lodging, nourishment, water, or attire.

Forlornness

CHAKRA AFFECTED heart chakra

At the point when we feel forlorn, we are under the feeling that we are not connected with anybody. This is an incredible inclination, and an amazing deception. Our heart chakra instructs us that we are altogether outfitted to adore and to connect with one another (indeed, even those of us who authenticate being mavericks!). Love is the genuine article, and anything taking after fear, (for example, depression, which is feeling separated or the fear of being detached) isn't. We all need to interface. Our heart chakra needs us to connect, not just with ourselves — the most significant connection of all— however with other individuals. At the point when we are really, profoundly forlorn, it is regularly on the grounds that the connection with ourselves has been lost. This is the domain of the heart chakra.

If you are feeling desolate, it might be on the grounds that the heart chakra is out of balance, and you may have cut off yourself from affection, regardless of whether as a response to being harmed in the wake of opening your heart or in light of the fact that you believe you don't merit love. At the point when we think that it's hard to give ourselves adoring grace, for example, setting aside the effort to do daily undertakings, performing self-care customs like resting when required, eating nourishments that fuel our system in sound ways, and encircle ourselves with elevating individuals, it is hard for our heart to emanate with bliss. At the point when we completely and totally love ourselves and are connected with our heart chakra, we are rarely really desolate, regardless of what our conditions.

Neck Pain

CHAKRA AFFECTED throat chakra

Neck pain that isn't brought about by physical injury or substantial damage (like a mishap) can be the aftereffect of imbalanced throat chakra energy identified with the manner in which we connect with the world. At the point when we neglect to convey what needs be in a genuine or open manner, or when we attempt to conceal certain pieces of ourselves, for example, fear or instability, from other individuals, it makes unbalanced characteristics in the throat chakra. Instances of this conduct may be professing to be glad in a relationship when where it counts, you're disappointed, or keeping yourself away from talking transparently at work.

There might be a scope of reasons why we keep ourselves down, yet the outcome is normally the equivalent—neck pain brought about by a failure to communicate uninhibitedly and straightforwardly.

Neuropathy

CHAKRA AFFECTED third eye chakra

Neuropathy, or feeling pain all through the body or in a particular region of the body. This is frequently the consequence of horrendous damage, disease, diabetes, reactions of chemotherapy, acquired causes, or introduction to poisons. However, if the reason isn't because of neurological damage, it might be the aftereffect of an imbalanced third eye chakra, on the grounds that this chakra can be connected with neurological aggravations. A case of this is encountering pain in the body subsequent to feeling detached from our instinct or fearing the psychological parts of ourselves. In many cases, fear of our profound self can demonstrate that we are either nearly getting progressively connected with our inward knowledge, or that we really have an extremely solid instinct and fear our capacity. In this way, if neuropathy is brought about by lively blockage, this might be shown by having the option to just concentrate on the acumen and coherent personality, dismissing any psychological points of view we may have, and concentrating just on what is physically before us — which are all parts of an unequal third eye chakra.

Panic Attack

CHAKRAS AFFECTED heart chakra, sun oriented plexus chakra, root chakra

Panic attack happen when we are held by unexpected, intense, and debilitating anxiety. They are regularly joined by palpitations, a beating heart, expanded pulse, perspiring, trembling, shaking, brevity of breath, and a feeling of approaching fate. These crippling assaults can happen when we are separated from our heart chakra and are not tuning in to what it's attempting to let us know. Furthermore, our root chakra is included when frenzy and fear set in, on the grounds that our base fear for our own endurance can be activated. With our heart chakra feeling separated and our fear systems in play, our capacity focus at the solar plexus chakra can feel like we've been punched in the gut, in light of the fact that our confidence and feeling of certainty lives there.

Sciatica

CHAKRAS AFFECTED root chakra, sacral plexus chakra

Sciatica is a pain condition that emanates from the lower back, through the hips and backside, and down every leg. At the point when it's not brought about by injury to the spine, or some other damage, sciatic pain can mirror an imbalanced root chakra. The root chakra manages issues around endurance and being.

At the point when basic issues emerge, similar to where you're getting your next dinner, in case you will have the option to make your lease, if your youngsters will be accommodated, or if you by and large live in fear that all the essential things in life might be effectively grabbed away, at that point your root chakra isn't in concordance.

Also, sciatica can emotionally symbolize fear of cash and what's to come. Whenever we have issues with pain that breaking points how we stroll in this world, actually and allegorically, we have to inquire as to whether we are deliberately constraining our advancement to push ahead throughout everyday life, or if we are living in fear of the subsequent stages that we may need to take to achieve our objectives.

Now and then when we experience sciatic pain, it might be on the grounds that we feel perilous in this world. The sacral plexus chakra is identified with the lower vertebrae, pelvis, and hip territory, so it might merit analyzing whether we are associating with and regarding our feelings, if we are unreservedly communicating inventively, and if we can enable ourselves to appreciate delight throughout everyday life.

Self-loathing

CHAKRAS AFFECTED heart chakra, root chakra, solar plexus chakra

Self-loathing depends on the discernment that we are unlovable—that we don't merit love because of accomplishing something we see as horrendous, or on the grounds that when we were more youthful, we were trained we were unlovable.

Accepting we are unlovable is an immediate consequence of separation from our heart chakra. The heart chakra is about adoration—love and sympathy for ourselves and for other people—and love consistently starts inside.

If we despise ourselves, which is an educated conduct dependent on obsolete discernments, we have to perceive how we came to accept that. Furthermore, detest is a furious energy and feeling. Also, anger consistently comes from fear.

Fear of our reality and the failure to defend ourselves are situated in the root chakra. Fear identified with self-loathing can also live in the solar plexus chakra, if it is fear because of absence of confidence. If this chakra is uneven, our capacity focus is tested, and we may feel an absence of certainty. In feeling frail, frightful of existing, and separated from our heart chakra, we can without much of a stretch accept obsolete observations that we are unlovable. The uplifting news is obsolete discernments are updateable, and energy can move rapidly to recalibrate.

Stomach Pain and Disorders

CHAKRA AFFECTED solar plexus chakra

Stomach pain and disarranges can come in numerous structures: ulcers, stoppage, looseness of the bowels, fiery inside disorder (IBS), colon/intestinal issues, heartburn, indigestion, and gastritis, among others. Beside eating something that legitimately arouses our stomach related tract, stomach pain can also come about because of feeling overpowered, crazy, weak, scared, or ailing in sense of pride. What we take in through our capacity focus (our solar plexus chakra) is a path for us to process our environment and take in our condition.

For instance, I once realized a patient who experienced scenes of indigestion after her separation. For this situation, her body was communicating the "acidic" feeling of disdain that the experience gave her. It was hard for her to process her separation, which had made her feel weak and crazy. Our bodies are continually letting us know precisely where our uneven characters falsehood, and stomach related issue are no exemption.

CHAPTER SIX

Healing Remedies and Treatments

Solar Plexus Chakra

The sunlight powered plexus chakra is among the most often obstructed chakras and may be the foundation of various essential grievances.

Why Fixing Solar Plexus Chakra Imbalances?

The sunshine powered plexus chakra, known in Sanskrit since Manipura, is your third chakra and can be located in the land of their navel and sun established plexus. It's just the chakra principally connected esteem, certainty and self-discipline.

A reasonable Manipura chakra allows you to get power over your concerns and passionate responses, place sound limitations, and discover a feeling of contentment on your own. Its bodily affiliation is with gut related capability.

The sun-based plexus chakra is called the "glistening pearl" energy focus within our own bodies because it sparkles brightly enjoy sunlight when corrected.

Have you at any stage experienced unbelievable certainty, freedom, and inward driveway on your lifetime? This was probably whenever your sunlight-oriented plexus chakra was strong, educated, and functioning during its perfect condition.

Be this as it might, there are various propensities, mentalities, and dreadful encounters in life which can lead to your sunlight predicated plexus chakra to become obstructed, stifled or rancid. In the event you have struck an Spartan youth, devoting, dictator guardians or characters during your lifetime, psychological, passionate, physical or sexual maltreatment or have been accommodated as a kid with undermining philosophies, (for example, rigorous, habitual or social responsibility), you probably have a hindered sunshine powered plexus chakra.

Indications of the Solar Plexus Imbalance:

Chakra unbalanced features happen as an overabundance of energy or an energy insufficiency. Side effects connected with above the top energy in sunlight established plexus chakra comprise:

- Assessing, bigoted, or even concentrated conduct
- Overeating and overindulgence
- Infection or foolish lethargy
- Manifestations of energy deficiency comprise:
- Insecurity, anxiety and dread
- Low body fat and Bad craving
- Insufficient certainty and bad mental Self-evident
- Inability to centre and sloppiness

- Indications of the Unhealthy Solar Plexus Chakra

Here are a couple of hints to cover:

- You constantly feel tired and lethargic
- You've got a problem with gorging and overindulgence
- You may generally restrain others to get exactly what you require, OR...
- You and feel weak and helpless
- You may generally be a domineering jerk or too commanding around the others, OR...
- You are feeling undependable and unassertive
- You will need self-assurance in several everyday problems
- You may generally look for endorsement from various other people (for instance you're an adapting individual)
- You've got low assurance, OR...
- You've got an unnecessarily swelled feeling of ego (for instance a significant character)
- Your system temperature is normally Freezing OR sexy
- You've got addictive propensities
- You struggle to ship limitations around other people
- You encounter the ill effects of some stomach related frame issue, as an instance, IBS, nausea, nausea, diabetes, obesity, etc.
- You encounter the effects of successive gasoline, obstruction or tummy upset
- You've got exorbitant load round the gut (for instance a bud gut)

Stomach ulcers, diabetes, eczema, dietary difficulties and distinct sicknesses connected to the gut related frame can similarly be signs of an unequal sunlight powered plexus chakra.

Directions to Heal Your Solar Plexus Chakra

Recuperating the sunlight-oriented plexus chakra is really a fundamental process, nevertheless it may require some instruction. The huge majority have grown a congestion over numerous decades; therefore chakra fixing will need a little investment. There are a few sunlight-based plexus chakra strengthening practices which are anything but hard to rehearse every day.

The chakra shading connected with Manipura is yellowish, meaning that carrots, citrus seeds, yellow peppers and peppers are excellent sun-based plexus chakra regaining nourishment. Flavours for your sun predicated plexus chakra are lavender, ginger, mint, and lavender.

Reflection can assist with launching Manipura. A fundamental exercise is to simply envision a glorious yellow sunflower on your sun predicated plexus chakra. This is sometimes considerably progressively compelling together with the usage of chakra stone. Sun established plexus chakra regaining stones include yellowish stones such as citrine, gold, yellow tourmaline and tiger's attention.

Fragrance Based therapy can similarly be practical to get Manipura chakra recuperating. It is inclined to be used while considering or performing yoga or without anybody else's present. Citrusy primary oils such as strawberry and strawberry are helpful for repairing sunlight plexus chakra, since are lavender, ginger and mint.

Regular Yoga training is ideal for chakra adjusting. Asanas that focus on centre quality are best for both Manipura recuperating. Warrior Pose is the toughest yoga asana for launching Manipura. Maintaining it for a few minutes every morning will begin to start your sun predicated plexus. Other inviting asanas have been Boat Pose (Navasana), which strengthens the middle, also Sun Salutations (Surya Namaskar). Participate in coordinated hazard taking through your yoga training, like performing a challenging position or tenderly depriving yourself longer, can similarly help equilibrium Manipura.

At long past, because the sunlight pushed plexus chakra is connected with the fire and sun, essentially getting outdoors can provide help. Reflecting or performing yoga out on sunny days will enhance your recovering practice, but basically going out for a walk or doing a little sunbathing can help open your sun-centred plexus chakra.

Here are most likely the very best sunlight powered plexus chakra strengthening practices on the market that will allow you to begin to fix this lively attention:

1. Break from regular and head out on a sidewalk

Most suitable insufficient blockages

Dormant and "secure" schedules only will generally spread our thoughts of frailty. Divide the dull sin of your own life and take a look at something new. Venture out of your everyday program and proceed exploring, irrespective of if that suggests setting off into another strip mall on your Saturday shopping excursion. Really, even small breaks in regular will blend you with energy and essence. One little change may provide you the inspiration and also re-established energy you want.

2. Cut ties with fundamental and negative people

Most suitable for insufficient and above the upper blockages

In the occasion you cannot cut ties eternally with negative and basic people, try your very best to maintain a good manners from these. During this great time, you are going to gain by continuous people who will encourage you to grow, not unsupportive people who can drag you through the mud. Remember that the energy is within your grip. It's determined by one to choose who stays and moves on your lifetime. If that someone is as frequently as possible endangering, underestimating, or castigating you, then find a means to divert them out of the life.

3. Explore the best sources of resistance on your lifetime

Most suitable for insufficient and above the upper blockages

What are you fighting against? What exactly are you afraid of? What problems hold coming your lifetime? At the stage when you pose such questions and discover the right reply, you're show the very best source of energy misfortune on your lifetime. The subsequent phase is to determine the way to conserve your energy and halt the barrier. Ask yourself, "What should I get, adore or forego that'll free my energy?" Many times, people who have obstructed sunlight established plexus chakras will generally contribute immense steps of energy towards combating, keeping up a strategic space away from or smothering something.

4. Eat a greater amount of those nourishments

Most suitable for inadequate and above the upper blockages

Eat grains, as an instance, oats, rice, spelt, and rye that are for the most part outstanding for processing. Take a peek at integrating more vegetables on your dietary plan, as an instance, lentils, chickpeas, and beans. Contain flavours, as an instance, ginger, garlic, cumin, and cinnamon for a nutrition since these tastes are warming to your system. Also, comprise of yellowish products of this soil, as an instance, oranges, carrots, carrot, carrot, and yellow capsicums to your eating program.

5. Get out from the sun more

Most appropriate for missing and above the upper blockages

As sunlight established plexus chakra is talked to from the part of passion, sunlight is an exceptionally repairing source of all essence. In fact, the nutrient D you've got in your own life, the more likely your problems, as an instance, uneasiness and wretchedness. Opting to get a fundamental morning walk in the daytime, or in any case, relaxing toward the day sunshine with a good cup of tea can be a wonderful practice for sunlight established plexus chakra.

6. Discharge any displeasure you shop inside

Most appropriate for insufficient and above the upper blockages

At the stage when performed connected with establishing, releasing repressed outrage can aid you with bettering your sun-based plexus fast. Our filthy power is often communicated as obstructed outrage (just consider the "mad" blasts of all volcanoes!), so if we release that outrage we could get to this energy once again.

Require a stab at releasing your outrage at a good fashion, for example, through playful exercise, hitting, kickboxing, moving, singing, writing, yelling or communication it via craftsmanship.

7. Require a greater amount of those purifying herbs

Most suitable for inadequate and surplus blockages

Use herbs to assist clear and ground the sun-based plexus, for example, rosemary, lavender, lemongrass, marshmallow leaf, and ginger.

8. Quit considering to be an "injured person"

Most suitable for insufficient blockages

One of the very damaging mentalities hauled by people with obstructed sunlight established plexus chakras is your thought that they're "delicate" and benign casualties of existence. In case you communicate this mindset, it is going to show since the propensity to reprimand different people on your despondency. You might also end up constantly affording your needs for different men and women, who do not typically value your jobs.

Furtively, there's a good deal of energy put into enjoying the individual in question, and it's a veneer that should be maintained up (and reaffirmed) daily. On the off likelihood that you consider to be a person who's being manipulated by someone else or something else, explore what it seems like to say "no." Playing with the unfortunate casualty is indeed attractive in light of how it empowers individuals to sidestep the heaviness of all self-duty, and therefore don't be amazed at the event you become startled of "venturing up" and regaining your own capacity. It requires training and boldness.

9. Repeat the corresponding assertions

Most suitable for inadequate and intense blockages

Recover your power by repeating the corresponding assertions: "I will," "I shall," "that I possess the capability to select," "I'm strong and daring," "I grip my calibre," "I love the person I am," "I go to bat to me personally," "I'm responsible for my entire life," "I'm worthy of affection and jealousy,"" I'm entirety." The further you recreate these attestations together with earnestness, the longer they'll revaluate your unaware character, and in such a fashion, start your sun established plexus chakra. Have a stab at start every morning with these confirmations.

10. Snicker on your own

Most suitable for insufficient and above the upper blockages

At The stage once we can giggle in ourselves and detect humour throughout daily life, we've got control. Really, the

110

darkest days of existence could be imbued with funniness. Cleverness is an outstanding source of both solidarity and informs us that existence is always in a state of change. Nothing really lasts as before! At the stage once we detect comedy, we detect chance. The more real you're, the further disengaged you're out of the source of strength.

11. Think with all the corresponding precious stones

Most suitable for inadequate and foolish blockages

Use precious rocks as emotional totems that will allow you to match your energy. Have a stab at ruminating or dispersing valuable stones, for example, gold, topaz, citrine, and tiger's eye, along with yellowish calcite.

12. Relinquish unfortunate relationships

Most suitable for missing and intense blockages

Undesirable connections are colossal sources of energy misfortune and are frequently responsible for sunlight centred plexus blockages and energy stagnation. Connections may be enthused, psychological, and also physical. We can become linked to criteria, convictions, recollections, needs, desires, fears, people, stains, things, and materials.

Connections are essentially kinds of energy that eventually become "trapped" in our brains and bodies. Now then, these pieces of energy gotten so thick that they result in poisonous addictions and badly constraining propensities.

The most perfect approach to split an undesirable relationship is by simply asking yourself, "Can this conviction/memory/want/thing serving my noteworthy amazing?" The moment it's possible to realize that something on your own life is drawback is that the moment which you're able to begin the process of recuperation. Offering up is tied with figuring out how to cope with yourself and locate internal security and strength without the necessity for an outside support.

13. Deal with yourself every day

Most suitable for insufficient and intense blockages

Audio confidence is just one of the bases of a lively sunshine established plexus chakra. At the stage when you handle your entire body and psychological health, your energy at a split moment winds up match. Contemplate what areas of your bodily, psychological, enthused or psychological wellbeing you've been disregarding. Also, think about what exactly is causing one of the most misery on your own life, and concentrate on that! For example, if the event you have been ignoring your entire body, it is going to reveal as throbs, distress, and incessant illness. If you have been blowing your heart, then you'll feel pressured, angry, or even overpowered.

Dealing with your self is a form of self-respect and value. Bear in mind, no individual may consider you superior to whatever you are able to. Only you understand your most deep wants at any and every given moment.

14. Work out How to inhale deeply and Earn a stride again

Most suitable for Unusual blockages

If that you struggle with controlling or controlling different people, work out how to focus on your breath. By breathing making a stride, you are able to ponder the position (and person) near. Concentrating in your breath may also provide you with the room to deal with yourself with compassion and also to comprehend any kind of internal self-growth is really a weep for consideration and affection.

15. Clear squares together with yoga

Most Suitable for inadequate and foolish blockages

Yoga is an extreme and rich strategy to reset your entire body and some other smothered vitality which may be placed away. For opening the sunlight- based plexus, try yoga stances, for example, the bow gift, upwards pooch, complete wheel gift, along with the breath of flame. It'd be perfect if you notice that if you try these yoga poses, you might encounter joys of energy that is ardent. Do your best not to worry; this energy is being discharged as a characteristic of this clearing process.

16. Do a sunlight-oriented plexus perception

Most suitable for insufficient and foolish blockages

Envision a spinning chunk of luminescent yellowish light on your gut. Feel that the chunk of energy that is fantastic dissolving all blockages or solid progressions of energy inside you.

17. Connect with yourself subject by defining goals

Most suitable for insufficient blockages

Conquer laziness by building a rundown of ten items you may want to attain and dedicate yourself to completing those items. This self-controller rundown may be mind boggling or fundamental as you would like. As an example, you need to enhance your posture, get more rest, begin a different eating plan, monitor your expenses, or see a particular book. By establishing clear goals, you'll have the choice to practice yourself discipline all the more efficiently.

18. Scrub sunlight established plexus chakra with basic oils

Most suitable for insufficient and above the upper blockages

Use Oils, for example, black pepper, cinnamon, lavender, cypress, clove, and sandalwood. It's possible to put these oils in an oil diffuser, rub them onto your wrist (at a diminished arrangement), or put them at a diffusing pendant.

At Long past, it is possible to similarly try to murmur "smash" yourself. The vibrations of the audio fit the vibrations of sunlight established plexus.

Heart Chakra

Heart chakra healing could be required while the heart attention is closed, and its energies are either obstructed or unequal. The heart chakra looks like a conductor to get a kind of energy that's ordinarily linked with adoration. At the stage once the energy of the centre chakra does not flow, an individual may strike it in different levels, from physical and emotional to existential. By adjusting the heart, an individual may experience a lift in energy, inspiration, love, compassion, and enlarged feeling of connectedness to existence.

What does regaining the centre chakra mean?

Healing the centre chakra may signify a couple of items and alludes to several processes. We'll ensure the principle kinds and remain as possible as can be enabled. Heart chakra regaining is in some instances also called fixing, starting, or draining. The basic thought behind regaining the heart chakra would be to re-establish flow of energy and generally talking parity.

Defenders of chakra regaining and adapting of those energies of this principle chakras, take this achieves fixing of dis-ease, unlocks the organic capabilities which we introduced into the world together, quiets the mind and prepares to detect deep harmony. We figure out the way to let life to flow, be energetic in regards to the endless presents that we're not conscious about. We come to comprehend that anxieties and issues don't to rule our waking hours like this paining the sub-conscious.

Through the heart we comprehend and acknowledge the importance of adoration unqualified love that's available to all. Since the heart chakra goes, it integrates another six important moves, brings to arrangement the bodily and the deep self, together these lines becoming life balance. Considering the heart chakra expands the significance of meditation words and deeds – it moves us to the real importance of adoration an overall and unequivocal love.

The heart chakra emanates command that induces us reside bounteous and fulfilling lives. It's a controlling energy that vents the bodily and psychological airplanes that assist us detract from behaving naturally concentrated, un-minding, feeling like an injured person and other unwanted traits. The heart chakra is the place we all pull plenitude within our own lives thus, we are able to exude this to other men and women. We discuss a planet past ourselves, we proceed beyond the apparent limitations of the physical universe, be mindful and aware that we're completely connected. That is harder than you might anticipate.

There are various kinds of expression. Dealing together with all the chakras is a considerate process together representation. You will find resources on the internet offering excellent reflective practice about the heart chakra.

For what reason would we want heart chakra regaining?

The heart chakra is particularly helpless against aggravations connected with love and connections. We as a whole have a last full of relations from the moment we are destined to now. Throughout our history, you will find many occasions and doors to get negative or positive experiences in regards to identifying and love with other people.

As we encounter life challenges, we have two key approaches to accommodate: we might close down or reduce the energy we devote to the position we might lift or construct our energy to combat it. These immunity components become moored within our mind.

On account of their heart, we could have felt hurt during childhood or a continuing separation and closed down our chakra to purify our distress and detract from distress. Or on the other hand, we might have stretched and opened our core vitality into a requesting accomplice or parent from chance, sometimes to the stage of over-broadening and being disoriented.

After some moment, these shield systems may lead to an unbalanced feeling from the heart and distinct chakras, causing an overactive, inadequate or obstructed area. An individual may will generally have prosperity or insufficiency at the heart area, or even both relying on the circumstance and process for handling anxiety.

118

When do you need to recover the heart: signs and symptoms?

At the stage once the heart needs healing could be motioned by means of a range of unwanted effects running out of the bodily to psychological.

Physical heart chakra signs

The fourth chakra is connected with all the part of atmosphere and is located in the torso territory. Therefore, a whole lot of the physiological side effects of coronary chakra unbalance state are directly connected with the cartilage, lungs, and heart disease. Look for the corresponding: hypertension, problems breathing, and disease in the amount of the lung, and oesophageal, heart disease.

Mental and emotional heart chakra signs

At the stage once the heart chakra is insufficient or closed, it may convert in the accompanying psychological and enthused traits:

- being hauled back
- avoiding social activities
- being too disparaging of other people and oneself
- lacking compassion
- feeling split

If that the centre chakra is too open, it may convert to:

- being overly asking of others, especially close household or accomplice
- extending to meet additional people' apparent has into the cost of a person's own equalization
- tendency to sense like an unfortunate casualty
- slimming feeling of person limits in a style that's bothering to a prosperity

Fixing and fixing the heart chakra

At the stage once the heart melts up incompetent, this could prompt emotional, physical or perhaps existential distress. The energy running yet this chakra is not flowing publicly and you might feel tired, tired, trapped in musings or private behaviour standards.

To overcome a congestion, overabundance or insufficiency at the heart area, the energy must:

- be prepared to proceed uninhibitedly (one might want to relax choking affects or impedances, for example, persistent stress, bodily muscle stress, improper dietary plan, negative effect of the others, constraining convictions or frame of mind)
- proceed at a pattern that's appropriate for this chakra
- be counter tops with unique energies (we have to consider the whole chakra and energy system; for

instance, anxiety or awkwardness in neighbouring overtraining can affect the state of this heart chakra)

Throat Chakra

At the stage we have a good throat chakra, we're innovative, honest, sure, self-assured, and unafraid of communication our reality into the planet.

Be this as it might, once we own a blocked throat we struggle with problems, as an instance, fear of communication meditations, timidity, social uneasiness, untruthfulness, obstinacy, conniving, lack of creativity, along with verbal forcefulness. Recollect your own adolescence in which you were probably convicted a ton by your own people or guardians? Did your household advocate you to express that truth? Are your meditations, ideas, and thoughts prestigious? If you had a tendency you could not straightforwardly state your musings and feelings, most likely, you struggle with an unwelcome throat.

This manual will let you begin your one of a type process of throat healing.

What is your Throat Chakra?

The throat, or Vishuddha, is your energy focus within our own bodies connected together with correspondence, fact, and also self-articulation. Located at the bottom of the throat, the throat chakra is linked to the shading blue along with the part of aether. This really is responsible for controlling the energy related with validity, creativity, and understanding.

What Can Be Throat Chakra Healing?

The Throat, otherwise referred to as the Vishuddha chakra, is your chakra of the body. Located at the bottom of the neck, that this energy focus is connected together with correspondence, inventiveness, and self-articulation. According to some deep and rigorous customs, the throat chakra is seen as the chair, or residence, of individual perception.

Consider it. At the stage once we are very angry, we often state we are "awakened," unfit to speak unmistakably, which communicates well when the throat is your passionate centre stage. Really?

Known as Vishuddha at Hindu habit, the throat chakra regulates the thyroid gland and endocrine system. That suggests it's responsible for the principle and flow of hormones and also the potential for all the issues of their throat and mind, such as:

- Trachea
- Mouth
- Oesophagus
- Teeth
- Nose
- Ears

- Carotid arteries

Throat chakra regaining is the action of starting, repairing, and optimizing the throat inside our own bodies. For the large part, throat recuperating uses a broad range of comprehensive healing options for transport arrangement to the entire body, mind, and spirit. These treatments include practices, as an instance, yoga, maintenance, shading therapy, audio adjusting, self-request, lively recovery, and many others.

21 Evidence of an Unhealthy Throat Chakra

The best approach to inform whether you need to experience throat recuperating is to pay attention to your meditations, feelings, actions, and bodily sensations within your own body.

Here are a couple of hints to cover exclusive head to:

- You believe that it's hard to express your emotions in a solid fashion
- you struggle to verbalize your meditations
- you're feeling apprehensive when trying to impart your own insights, or...
- you may generally push your evaluations onto other people
- you combat a ton with miscommunication on your relations
- you always feel ignored or misjudged by other people

- you retain a whole lot of insider facts from other people due to a paranoid fear of never being confessed
- you are feeling on edge in talks
- you're shy around others
- you believe that it's hard to be your own bona fide self
- you may generally be over-stubborn, or ...
- you struggle to possess your own voice
- you are feeling almost incapacitated when doing open discussing
- you frequently enter restrictive links which don't allow you to voice your meditations and thoughts without becoming inspected
- you believe that it's difficult to be simple with yourself as well as some other people
- your actions fight with your words
- you've got swollen lymph hubs on your neck
- your voice much of the time breaks or sounds meagre
- you encounter the effects of hypo or hyperthyroidism
- you've got ear problems, by way of example, premature hearing obstruction or contaminations
- you produce regular sinus, throat or upper respiratory contaminations

How to rip the throat chakra?

Fifth chakra healing may incorporate using a range of devices to achieve equilibrium, from naturally occurring stones and fundamental oils into repairing nourishments, yoga asana (pose), manifestation and purging. It's crucial to recollect the idea behind adjusting would be to eliminate the pessimism that resulted in the awkwardness; that is normally an overabundance or inadequacy of something.

One of the most commonly used tools for neck healing are neck chakra stones.

So how do stones function exactly? It is about shaking.

We are completely made from vitality. Vitality creates shaking. When chakras become irregular, a coming into the suitable vibration is vital. Chakra adjusting stones each possess their particular vibrational recurrence. By placing throat chakra stones just above or over the corner of unevenness,

Recuperating that the throat chakra with colour: true blue

Each among the seven individual chakras have their very own concerning shading. Blue is connected to the throat chakra. Thought about a tone for both purging and health, gloomy calming influence re-establishes stability and eases physical and psychological burdens often connected with throat awkwardness.

Benefits of fifth chakra balance

At the stage once the throat is corrected, you're feeling that, however there are additional, unobtrusive signals. You've got more certainty and find you're a progressively successful communicator. Also, you might discover that you have progressively striking fantasies and fantasy inspection, are increasingly touchy into the energies placed forth by other people around you, and also therefore are somewhat more serene with all the world all whatsoever.

Third Eye Chakra

An Open third eye chakra lets you think about items to be that they really are, nevertheless even the scarcest instability may unleash jealousy in your own mental, enthused, and physiological health.

Indigo is the most frequently recognized type shading linked to the Third Eye. What's more, silver, purple and colours of darkest blue/purple can similarly be used.

Third Eye Imbalance

At the stage as soon as the third eye chakra produces plenty of energy the mind can enter overdrive. Consider how you are feeling after having too much of cups of espresso and you receive the notion. An overactive Ajna chakra will make it tough to believe as well as now and can begin mind clocks.

On the opposite end of this scope, a power inadequacy can similarly influence your capability to concentrate on, process and remember information. An underactive Third Eye chakra can cause you to be reluctant, postpone, or be terrifying of this vague. Unbelievably lacking Ajna chakra capability can upset your capability to centre, maintain a calm mind under stress, or fantasy and review your own dreams.

Extra Problems that could emerge out of a blocked or imbalanced Third Eye chakra comprise:

128

- Insomnia
- High circulatory strain
- Sciatica
- Depression
- Stress
- Migraines

Measure By step directions to Activate Your Third Eye Chakra

Chakra manifestation is a basic bit of launching the Ajna chakra.

There are many online aides about the way to begin the Third Eye Chakra utilizing chakra fixing manifestation. Regardless of the plan you select, recollect the crucial elements to profitable chakra healing meditation and chakra exciting incorporate being loose, understanding, and heart interest.

The idea behind stimulating the Third Eye, or eyebrow, chakra would be to observe matters all the more unmistakably (indoors and with no physiological domain) and also to stir your own instinct. Bear in mind, that the Ajna chakra operates in business together with the crown chakra to complete the chakra "circuit" When the Ajna chakra is awakened and functioning in tandem with the crown chakra a different amount of mindfulness could be cultivated.

Third Eye Chakra Healing

Beside Chakra meditation, there are a couple unique strategies to re-establish stability to a Third Eye chakra, for example, usage energy mending, for example, Reiki, audio therapy, needle treatment or pressure point massage.

In the occasion which you are a yoga pro, you will find asanas which may help using Third Eye chakra regaining and correcting, such as child's position, shoulder stands, and even forwards spins.

Fusing using basic oils, for example, to bless the eyebrow at the locale of the Ajna chakra, may similarly aid with purging and correcting the Third Eye chakra. Consider using:

- Marjoram
- Frankincense
- Juniper
- Clary Sage
- Rosemary
- Sandalwood

Use healing stones which possess the equivalent vibrational recurrence and chakra shading since the Ajna chakra to collect up pessimism and revive proper energy flow, as an instance,

- Amethyst
- Lapis Lazuli
- Purple Flourite
- Moonstone

130

- Quartz

Chakra Fixing Food for Your Third Eye

Diet supposes an essential job on your overall wellbeing, such as your chakra frame.

To fix and maintain a solid Ajna chakra, consider purple. Ordinarily dim blue and black purple-shaded nourishments will assist Third Eye chakra capability such as:

- Eggplant
- Plums
- Blueberries
- Purple berries, cabbage, and kale

Nourishments That Assist Balance The Third Eye Chakra

Chakras are your potential supply. They're spots on your body where your coated energies are gathered. They're open doors indefinitely capacity to flow into and from your own emotions. They discover your hesitance and maintain your soul. In the event they are discharged things considered it looks nourishment for your soul. They're just like a power station, toward the conclusion of that can be rigorous lighting. At the time that your chakras are available, you can distinguish your truth into a lotus blossom. Even though a lotus blossom sprouts attractively in sand, in like way your life also flourishes if your chakras are revived. Third eye chakra is a source of strength for instinctive and monitoring sees.

Conclusion making is essential for anybody and you need to ensure he has this capability and use it also using brightness. In the event you are facing different issues with your capacity to repay on conclusions all things considered it's been exceptionally proposed that you ought to be incredibly mindful of third eye popping. The third eye chakra discharging is going to be necessary in this kind of situation all together, which everything could be return to the standard level that may be seen as useful. The rear rub techniques are anticipated to be unfathomably notable using the third eye popping opening as you can definitely accomplish glorious focal points onto it. In the event you are worried about your own life and you're anxious to secure improved results with fantastic choices everything considered you need to create identifying back rub methods for third-party opening.

The 6th chakra is inhabited with the understanding and making of ability and at the affirmation that which you see influentially impacts you. Even though your two eyes watch that the material ground, your 6th chakra sees beyond your physical. This film consists of clairvoyance, particular insight, imagining, intuition, creative thoughts and perception. Too much energy from the Third Eye Chakra can reach psychological distress, challenges concentrating, poor dreams, and psychological trips. A bad 6th chakra can provide ascent to inadequate memory and eye problems. Lemon juice and red wine would

132

be the most commonly known and most adapting nourishments for correcting third eye chakra, thus If that anyone should correct their next chakra, in the point endeavour to eat these kinds of foods convenient and routinely.

If that you're anxious to make certain that you live a happy life that may be packed with pleasure all things Considered among the very crucial highlights is mixing your third eye chakra. Just like your body needing sustenance, proteins, nutrients to keep moving in like fashion your chakras also anticipate nutrition to become well-fed and Noise and also to be more balanced. The food resources which you can incorporate to correct and encourage your next eye chakra include veggies and dark blue natural products, such as blackberries, blueberries and eggplant, helps energize the Third Eye Chakra. Lemon juice and red wine may also help animate your visual awareness, including poppy blossom and seed oil.

Crown Chakra

The seven chakras will be the targets that energy moves through from the entire body. At the stage when open and corrected, energy moves unreservedly via them and deep and bodily recovering can occur. Therefore, even once the chakras become obstructed, it can result in psychological and bodily malady. A congestion at the crown chakra might prompt deep disquietude and unique troubles.

Recognizing That the Crown Chakra

The crown chakra, called Sahasrara at Sanskrit, is the major chakra. It's located on the top of their head and can be connected with otherworldliness. The Sahasrara chakra is white or purple and can be associated with a lotus blossom with a thousand petals. This chakra is something that permits people to move beyond individual materialistic should connect with all the most inclusive entirety. Introduction the crown chakra attracts psychological understanding, maintenance and the capability to live with serene fearlessness in most sections of life.

Negative Consequences of Sahasrara Imbalance

A deficiency from the crown chakra will generally reason inconspicuous, principal difficulties. These include:

- Depression and psychological haze

- Persistent weakness
- Migraines and other ceaseless cerebral pains
- Greed and dishonesty

An abundance of energy from the crown chakra may similarly cause difficulties such as:

- Sensitivity to light and noise
- Neurological or endocrine matter
- Boredom and disappointment
- A sense of elitism or unmerited Accomplishment

An unbalanced crown chakra might similarly assume work in studying inabilities, trance conditions, rest problem, and mental maladjustment.

Healing that the Crown Chakra

The most dominant strategy to fix the crown chakra is via meditation. This is due to the ties between the crown and otherworldliness. Regular meditation regular with respect to several forms is gainful. To get a meditation focused on Sahasrara, envision white light fulfilling the maximum stage of your mind, filling your entire body and linking you with your overall environment. If that you have a few moments to consider, take a peek at envisioning a purple lotus blossom on your crown to get a simple chakra manifestation.

Dissimilar to various chakras, the crown chakra does not have some fixing nourishment explicit for this. This is an immediate effect of its own job in deep sustenance. Maintaining the entire body with wholesome, solid nourishments while focusing on deep items can help fix this particular chakra.

Quietness is most effective for crown chakra enactment, as it doesn't distract from deep practice. The sound of Om and deep, tonal noises may similarly be healing songs for Sahasrara in light of the nature that is prevalent.

Most yoga asanas are useful for crown chakra adjusting in light of the reflective outlook. Slow practice which allows time for a whole lot of spotlight about the breath is ideal. This is not a perfect chance to push constraints and endeavour to achieve troublesome stances, nevertheless, rather to take care of maintenance and meditation.

Using chakra stones, as an instance, Selenite, Clear Quartz, Amethyst and Diamond can similarly be a feasible process to recover from crown chakra.

Fragrant healing for your crown chakra provides a broad range of scents. Elegant primary oils such as lavender, lavender and rose can ease an overactive crown, whereas artificial fundamental oils such as sandalwood, frankincense and myrrh will help re-establish an underactive or obstructed Sahasrara.

The crown chakra's elements are believed and mild, therefore investing energy from the daytime is helpful for opening the crown chakra. Perusing or performing confounds out on a luminous day is an easy approach to help fix the crown chakra.

Nourishments Nourish The Crown Chakra

Since your crown chakra is imperceptible, you need to always find out the way to nourish this and it is really for the most part dictated by the way you eat. Through fasting, this particular bit of your deep being constantly reverberates suitably in respect to the prerequisite explanation and also filtration. This information is important in light of how it determine the way your wealth affects your crown chakra. Hence, these are different ways about the way you should consume in order to keep this up chakra: always avoid nourishment with extra compounds and other added counterfeit fixings. These include all sugars which are imitation, additives, colours, and food colourings. These sections are always the source of toxic quality inside your body that arouses congestion of deep vitality diverts within the human physique. At the stage when this occurs, you might end up with some side effects, as an instance, hyperactivity, poor heart health, and also unexplainable brain illnesses.

Another part of your nourishments to get Sahasrara is you should always incorporate some fragile and important detoxes on your everyday nourishment stuffs. All these detoxes are meant to wash your body especially by expelling all toxins kept on your inner stations. These toxins may somewhat much be regarding the nutrition you consume, nevertheless additionally to unique factors like contaminations and being more inactive. Thus, you should always grasp nourishments which are rich in fibre. These include items such as leafy fruits, vegetables and distinct berries.

Ahead to carrying your healthy foods, you ought to allow it to be an ongoing point to always relax, consider and also consider how system and purgings that you should get. Continuously possess a brief request that should be for expressing appreciation toward everything befell the nature before that nutrition came into existence. This is essential especially in recognizing each of these interconnections behind this nutrition you're likely to take.

Aside in the normal nourishment stuffs, your crown chakra wants other rare kinds of nourishments. One of those nourishments will be daylight. Sun been one of the sources of overall energies, always results in the crown chakra into vibrate and interrogate suitably. This is important particularly with respect to sustenance of both adoration, elegance that's heavenly and also trust. Apart from the daytime, oxygen has also been a substantial nutrition for crown. Oxygen is essential especially with respect to both consciousness and lifestyles of chakra. As a consequence, you will always require this oxygen in order to maintain the viability of your crown chakra. At last enjoy is just another section your crown chakra worth. This affection needs to be predicated to all around you include

138

character, self-respect, and love of other people, ultimately adore of world. When you stick to each one of those guidelines to the Sahasrara nourishments, you may love the very best and perfect sanitizations and interconnectivities interior always.

Crown Chakra Meditations

The seventh and final chakra is the crown chakra. The crown chakra is the doorway to the institution together with the heavenly. Here you'll see association and insight with all animals of production.

Even though there are a variety of meditation, lighting, and chakra fixing will not specifically concentrate on the crown chakra. I'll provide you such manifestation that has been educated to me during the years.

Notice that opening the crown chakra may be a wonderful thing and you can quickly put some space between their real realities. A highly moderate and controlled grow of rehearsing this expression is definitely prompted.

Currently, I propose having seven identifying hued tangles or towels nearby that every talk to one of the seven chakra colours. Due to this crown chakra, the sealing is more violet. Along these lines, then possibly put your purple up tangle, or find a ribbon towel.

When you have spread your tangle outside, choose a sitting posture and then fold your legs Indian fashion. Otherwise referred to as the lotus position.

Next, we'll begin with starting to breath. At the first location, tenderly shut your eyes. With your eyes closed, look up below your eyelids. Currently, centre round carrying in and exhaling from numerical cases. For example, If that you breath for 3 minutes, breath for a mere 3 minutes.

When you've achieved a covert authorities of breathing which not expects one to should focus on it, slowly increase your arms over your mind. An adequate visual portrayal of the possibility of being an official in a soccer match-up flagging an "adequate" field goal kick.

With your arms from the skies, cup your palms. With all these cups, we will grab the purple blossoms our minds eye is watching and producing.

Sometime using just a tiny obstruction, begin to push down the blossoms to your crown and familiarize them with your crown chakra. Cease the palms at about 3 to 5 minutes on your face and maintain there for around 10 minutes.

As you wrap the position, slowly re-stretch your arms out to the start position. Repeat this for 12 reiterations in almost any instance. As you are feeling progressively great with all the profundity by this frees you out of the obvious fact, you might construct the redundancies into a pleasant level. Close to fifteen consecutive minutes should be led each arrangement.

Finally, employ a soggy heated substance for your closed eyes to loosen them up.

Manifestations of a Closed Crown Chakra

Brainwave entrainment a logically established neuro-innovative apparatus that acquaints explicit noise heartbeats together with the brain in a repeated and cadenced manner, with the goal of changing its existing brainwave recurrence to this of this increase, may break down the reflections of a closed and unequal Crown Chakra.

The mind will generally imitate this increase and resound the specific recurrence which can actuate the crown chakra, taking into consideration a quick and enduring evaluation, of its attributes.

The crown chakra talks to the collecting of heaven and earth and the reconciliation of itself with all the inner identity and is where deep arousing is begun.

Manifestations of a closed crown chakra include:

- Spiritual institution is simply exemplary, and you do not have a belief of being related to the source or when there's a supply.

- You forlorn and reject assistance from other people, depending without anybody else astuteness to finish things.
- You're joined into this material world and don't own a belief of satisfaction.
- Something is absent on your lifetime and you cannot find the right answers.
- You're sincerely numb.
- You accuse your problems without getting enough of something from the physical universe.
- Your action is not fulfilling.
- You always ask, "Is that all there is?"
- Since you're unhappy, you might leave your family and friends, partner, work, house... From the quest for bliss.
- Your otherworldliness is not near home.
- You do not have religion in post-existence.
- Your life wants significance and motive.
- You think you do not impact anyone.
- You've got psychological sadness.
- You fear the boring.
- You think you've been deeply deserted.
- You've lost person character and with culture.
- You've got cerebral brokenness.
- You will experience psychosis.
- You will experience the ill effects of epilepsy, Parkinsons disease, Alzheimers disease, multiple sclerosis, or fibromyalgia.
- You've discombobulated sessions.

- You're attracted to light, strong, and also the ground.
- You wait to serve your personal person.
- You're physically exhausted.
- You will experience a bone problem.

- You truly feel shaky, constantly discovering things... Particularly on a single side.
- You might think suicide and may be powerless against malignancy along with other critical infections.
- You're happy, haughty, along with a narcissist.
- You encounter difficulty learning matters and recollecting that which you realized.
- You're unhappy and have low assurance.
- You are feeling misjudged.
- You exhibit no lots of pleasure.
- You will pull back in the planet and be tremendously hostile to societal.
- You're a magnet for mysterious assaults and might end up in an institution as you're able to be efficiently controlled by negative power however you're going to be examined as maniacal.
- Your dread freezes you.

Offsetting the crown chakra with quartz crystal singing bowl meditation

The note connected with the crown chakra is b and its own shading is purple. For your quartz prized stone singing jar meditation, it's crucial to get one which is an e note stone singing bowl because of this manifestation to operate, because every chakra has its own vibration. It is not persuasive substitute different notes to the identical chakra.

To begin, put aside a couple minutes of time when you'll be constant and also make yourself as pleasant as could be wise. You can be located or placing down - it's altogether your decision. Strike your singing jar several occasions to flag the beginning of your own reflection. Now run the striker round the border and get started enjoying the bowl, making sure the noises develop into a constant, darkened even tone. Slow down your breathing to a constant, even speed, creating a stage to inhale deeply and totally.

As you breathe, feel relinquishing each one of your anxieties and being completely loose over the exhale. Imagine your crown chakra introduction along with also a fantastic light entering your body through the crown chakra and also spilling down throughout the rest of the entire body. Feel yourself getting an ideal satisfaction and bliss because this mild washes by you. Wait for thirty minutes and following that picture a second surge of light penetrating you. Repeat this process for a few minutes, stopping in the event which you feel dizzy or experience another type of distress.

You can similarly repeat attestations to yourself through or following this reflection. Some crown chakra connected certificates are:

- I'm supernaturally guaranteed and guided.
- I'm sheltered and life loves and bolsters me today.
- I expect entirely in spirit to prove to me my following stage.
- I'm merged with spirit and each single-family matter.

With coaching and tireless exertion, using these approaches together with your quartz stone singing bowl will make sure to offer you an open, flowing crown chakra and nearly all its favourable deep gifts.

CHAPTER SEVEN

Extra Techniques To Use Crystals, Meditation, And Yoga

CRYSTALS

Crystals have a sorted out geometric course of action of the molecules and in view of their organized structure they are in a condition of flawlessness. They transmit a solid rational energy, which reverberates with the existence power. They have energy fields, which impact man's electromagnetic field and can store different recollections. In the event that they stay in an unclean domain, their fiery recollections become hazardous as they emanate the negative energy that was put away inside them. Crystals can change the cerebrum waves if they are put on an energy focus - a reality confirmed with an Encephalogram instrument. If they are set on acupuncture centers, the skin obstruction changes, which demonstrates their capacity to change electric charges.

Crystals have the property of engrossing electromagnetic energy, store it, change it, and discharge it. They also can stimulate body and soul. They make negative particles that reinforce the energy of the body. The utilization of brilliant crystals and crystals is thusly suggested. Continuously spotless the crystals before use, by absorbing them for one hour a blend of half liter of water, a spoon of ocean salt, and a spoon of juice vinegar.

In performing treatment with gems, our mentality towards the crystals is significant. Sending it our affection and having confidence in the results it produces is significant. Use a Tiger-eye stone or Jasper stone to expand your energy. Request that the precious stone improve your energy, while holding it in your left receiving hand. In the event that there should be an occurrence of strain, the vast majority utilize the Aquamarine precious stone. The dark Tourmaline and Amber are fit for engrossing the body's cynicism. Each precious stone works in an alternate way. It is possible to increase the pace of vibration at home and ward off negative impacts by setting crystals at the sides of the rooms - quartz or Amethyst groups. In "Atlantis," the lost mainland a gem was introduced in each house and its capacity was to refine the air. Individuals in Atlantis utilized crystals to improve the sun's energy and this means that they didn't need any other source of fuel.

Wearing a precious stone around our neck enacts the thymus organ and the invulnerability system. It ought to be underlined however, that the precious stone increases the vibration it gets numerous falls. If somebody is irate, the gem will build his resentment. While wearing the precious stone or utilizing it you ought to make sure to be in condition of affection and empathy so the gem will expand these positive characteristics.

Each gem has its specific trademark. Ruby influences love and Jade influences intelligence. Individuals are attracted to gems due to their exceptional attributes. Crystals encapsulate enormous forces, offering them to the individuals who wear them. However, albeit valuable stones and crystals may pass on their qualities, one ought not depend on only them. They won't "carry out the responsibility" for us. They are fit for moving astronomical energy to us and we can utilize them similarly as an instrument to support us. If we wish to make progress with crystals, they ought to turn out to be a piece of us - part of our internal life. It isn't sufficient just to wear them, it is great to see them every now and then and fuse their qualities in us. Individuals are attracted to them since they get and transmit the light.

While cooking food decreases the levels of energy it emits. In the event that we place nourishment on a precious stone board, we add energy to it. Stone containing iron oxide or a quartz precious stone, one and half inch long in a liter of water during the night - improve the trial of the water and twofold its energy. It is great to put crystals or red hued stones in pockets, in work area drawers, and in organizers. They add energy to fabrics and cloth, while being put away. Precious stone sheets under a bundle of roses can extend the bloom's life. Crystals lessen pain, recuperate the body and diminish physical and mental pressure. That is the reason crystals are utilized as a helping instrument in clairvoyance, meditation and healing.

Programming a precious stone – crystals can be modified to help us. Above all else, you need to send love to the precious stone, hold it near your heart until you feel its closeness. Later on, place it on your temple, where the Third eye should be. Find in your creative mind the activity that the gem needs to accomplish for you and envision that your thoughts are entering the gem. Its activity is subject to your capacity to focus and all alone contact with it. Thank the precious stone consistently, for its fruitful activity and find in your creative mind how the final product is accomplished. In the event that someone contacts the precious stone, it is important to purge it with water and ocean salt and modified once more. The purifying of the gem is done also by consuming incense of cedar and salvia.

Meditation with a precious stone – sit down restfully with a straight back, holding the gem in the getting hand, the correct hand with many people. Watch the precious stone and reach it through your heart. Attempt to relate to it, gradually, gradually. Close your eyes and attempt to believe, to detect the precious stone with every one of its qualities - its temperature, its edges, its feelings and its shading. It is critical to open up to the gem's energy, which you can feel like warmth, cold or a jerk, and empower the energy to dispel in your entire body. Envision that you are the gem that turns straightforward increasingly more in each passing minute, gets information from the earth and draws in magnificence, harmony and serenity.

Balancing the two sides of the brain with crystals it is possible to adjust the two mind's sides of the equator with the guide of gems. Grasp a twofold ended precious stone and being in a reflective state, inhale air in your lungs. Exhale gradually, amass in your correct mind's side of the equator and close your left hand. Inhale again, keeping in mind that exhaling focus to your left side cerebrum's side of the equator - shutting your correct hand. Repeat this activity a few times. Taking care of issues with the guide of crystals - If you feel anxious, it is great to hold a smoky quartz gem, to contact the earth with it and relax. Later on, you should hold a straightforward precious stone with two hands, announce so anyone might hear your concern, in a raised voice - attempting to consolidate your concern into the gem. You should consolidate the issue in the precious stone and after that clean the gem from its vibration in water and ocean salt. Toss the water with the gem's vibration into the ground and envision that there it is changed. This activity is utilized as a helper apparatus to take care of your concern, by accelerating the conscious and the intuitive to act.

Healing with crystals- Use crystals as a helper apparatus in playing out the treatment of breathing, sounds and hues. Quartz ($SiO2$) is located in the body's cells, and influences them, as its energy fields and vibration coordinate our own. In the event that you need to utilize a precious stone for self-healing: relax in a helpful sitting position, or in lying position. Focus on the infected organ, the hurt spot and spot a precious stone on that spot or hold it in a natural way. You may utilize one precious stone or a blend of two crystals or a few gems. Normally it is prescribed to use at any rate two quartz gems, with one end, and a length of at any rate two inches each. One is held in the left hand towards the impact point of the hand, the other one in the correct hand, with its end coordinated towards the fingers. This situation of the crystals enables the energy to flow, considering that the correct hand emanates, while the left hand is getting. From the outset you simply envision the progression of energy, however after some time, you will feel the progression of energy, spilling in your body and the infected organ.

Crystals impact monstrously the energy centers. Red and orange crystals are utilized to reinforce the essence, blue and green crystals to re-establish the body and violet stones are utilized for psychological improvement. It is prescribed to put the crystals and crystals with the correct shading, on the different energy centers: blue on the throat, green on the heart. Something very similar works when we put them on our photo, or the photo of somebody we wish to fix. The photo has a similar vibration of the man envisioned in it. The technique works great. It is great to check with a pendulum the period of time the crystals should remain on the photo.

A Quartz gem on the Root's chakra brings a feeling of confidence, into our daily life. A Quartz precious stone on the Sexual chakra encourages us in sexual connections and brings essence. On the Solar plexus it illuminates our character. A man, who looks for places of intensity for himself, must offset the Solar plexus with philanthropy - the thought of other individuals' prosperity. A Quartz gem set on the Heart chakra purges our affection and increases our internal power. On Throat chakra it delivers expert articulation and clearness to our discourse. On the 6th chakra, it clears our thoughts, balances the two mind halves of the globe and upgrades the power over the psychological body. Set on the seventh chakra, the precious stone upgrades correspondence with the profound world and encourages the individual sense of self to join with the "Higher Self." A Quartz precious stone put on a chakra with its honed end towards our head filters the chakra. The amethyst stone frees us from material reliance and gets in touch with us with our imaginative forces. Amethyst stones, set on each chakra in the body, and one between the legs, help to connect with the Soul. Sapphires guarantee peacefulness and serenity and fortify our confidence.

Sea green/blue stones empower us to increase our healing power. With the help of seven Rose quartz stones we can get closer to the best righteousness - to unequivocal love. Garnet stones bring bliss and energy, and Amber stones bring achievement. If you wish to get healing energy inside 24 hours, place your or another person photo (if a photo is inaccessible, you may put hair or much finger-nails rather) on Agate board or a level quartz, on which you have included little green gems, in the state of a Star of David and a gem in the Star of David.

Pink and Green crystals are utilized for affection; violet crystals are utilized for otherworldliness. Crystals are source of energy and excellence and are utilized for:

1) Healing.

2) Massaging the reflex centers in the body, legs and hands.

3) Treating suitable acupuncture centers (with a Quartz precious stone three times each day).

4) Water, in which you place a gem for three hours, is useful for drinking and can be utilized for getting ready wet gauzes, or for a shower.

5) Crystals put on energy centers – help to open up blockages and are a guide for profound improvement.

6) To adjust the chakras, place the seven crystals that have a place with the chakras (see the outlines at the section of the chakras) in a straightforward glass in the moon light during the night and the sun during the day, and. Drink a spoonful of water once per day.

7) Crystals are utilized as a special necklace. Wear them on the body, on the materials, or put them even underneath the pad.

8) You may put them on all aspects of the body that needs to experience an activity, before the activity and after it. The precious stone's attributes are subject to their synthesis, size, virtue, shape and shading. In this manner, a watermelon Tourmaline is amazing for the Heart chakra, a pink Tourmaline fortifies the capacity of insight, a green Tourmaline sedates and dark Tourmaline grounds us and shields us from negative vibrations.

The following are the characteristics of some of the crystals:

Straightforward Quartz - purges, expands the faculties and blesses all the unpretentious bodies with energy.

Crystals and straightforward Quartz are energy intensifiers.

Garnet - fortifies the body, the blood, and is utilized against pains, discouragement and apprehensive depletion.

Lapis Lazuli - builds mental power. It is productive for the throat energy focus, helps clear self-expression in discourse, expands fearlessness and improves rest.

Lazurit - loosens up the muscles. It is useful for torn ligaments, for stomach and back issues.

Malachite - can draw out pain and it is prescribed for blood treatment, the liver, nerve bladder, hurting joints and stiffness.

Ruby - is suggested for stomach, belly and entrail issues, and wipes out toxic substances.

Opal - is being utilized against looseness of the bowels and against a sleeping disorder (by putting it underneath the cushion).

Amethyst - sedates and it is utilized against a sleeping disorder, thyroid issue and for profound elevating.

Obsidian and calcite - treat bones, inclined to breaking for absence of calcium, anticipate osteoporosis.

Citrine - is a tissue regenerator, purifying, growing and balancing the energy of the body and the emanation.

Topaz - accelerates moderate working organs, accelerates energy centers and discharges adrenaline into the blood. It is utilized against a sleeping disorder, depletion and thrombosis.

Kunzite - purifies antagonism, bringing balance and steadiness.

Jade - stimulates the blood flow, the mind's activity, is nerve - reinforcing and is useful for the heart, liver and kidneys.

Magnetite - emanates attractive energy, captivates the Yin and Yang energies.

Moldavit - rises vibrations and illuminates the spirit.

Tektite and Boji stones - adjusts, balances out and cleans the whole atmosphere and the chakras systems.

To cause a buzz of quietness and harmony utilize a Sapphire. Lapis Lazuli and Tourmaline widen the awareness. Quartz and Meteorite help to create inestimable awareness, Tourmaline bolster representation.

Precious stone and Beryl bolster clairvoyance, Hekimar jewel and Opal are utilized for knowledge and perceptiveness, topaz for internal quality and Jade for insight.

Meditation

Chakra meditation is an incredible method to improve your profound health and prosperity. By doing chakra meditation, you change your energy. At the point when you change your energy, you feel good, however it might also assist you with moving ahead on your way more effectively.

That is the reason chakra meditation can be extraordinary for when you feel obstructed somehow or another. Keeping your energy perfect and flowing encourages you to link with a more significant level of vibration. Your Self and the Universe (God, Higher Source, and so forth) convey all the more effectively in light of the fact that the universe doesn't need to experience all the vigorous garbage that is amassed in your energy system.

The homeostasis is simply the body's normal balance and submerging in Reiki Meditation can enable you to accomplish impeccable parity. The body's needs energy to recuperate, and through this meditation that energy can really originate from other individuals. There are various healing systems that are consolidated together to frame Reiki Meditation. It has been built up that the underlying foundations of meditation originate from the Vedic age. The Vedic individuals used to rehearse these strategies to mollify their divine beings, which they used to fear and love. There has been some discussion on its reality before the Vedic age too. In different ancient human advancements, there have been hints of these systems being utilized to connect with the maker of this world, by redundantly reciting certain musical melodies.

156

This routine with regards to interacting with your consciousness is a delightful inclination. Daily rehearsing these techniques makes you flawless and quiets your mind, body and soul. Today our everyday lives are loaded with weights, duties and bedlam. There is no space for meditation and meditation. The tension builds so much that individuals get discouraged, pushed and disturbed effectively. You will seldom run over an individual who is by all accounts glad and isn't experiencing pressure. By rehearsing meditation, you can explore through every one of these issues.

For what reason do Chakras become Clogged Up?

You are a vigorous being. Your thoughts and feelings are also energy. Chakras become stopped up with cloudy looking, slow, thick energy when we have musings and feelings that are brimming with self-analysis, delayed displeasure, delayed blame - all the negative kinds of energies that we by and large attempt to shield ourselves from falling into.

Your physical body can also influence how your chakras are working. It is usually accepted that your thoughts, feelings and physical wellbeing are altogether interconnected.

I've seen individuals who are debilitated whose energy system is dim, powerless, little, and overcast. I've also observed chakras in fluctuating conditions of wellbeing - from being little and by and large brilliant, to strangely formed, dull in shading, colossal and splendid, light and glad inclination, dim and substantial.

These are for the most part impressions of the individual's perspective, feelings and physical wellbeing. Pessimistic feelings, nourishments that are not beneficial, stress, being encompassed by adverse individuals - every one of these things can begin to influence the nature of the vibration of your energy.

These will in general be lower recurrence, more slow influxes of energy that you may assimilate or bring into your energy system. At the point when this occurs, it begins to meddle with how your chakras can process energy. That is when chakras get stopped up and may begin to get blocked.

Eight Ancient Guided Medication Techniques to Know!

These 8 antiquated methods have been around for more than a huge number of years and have stood the trial of time. Seeing every meditation process will give you a diagram of the aim and reason for the apparatus to enable any fledglings to move beyond the underlying obstacles to realize inward harmony inside, while simultaneously discharge worry to advance healing for the mind and body.

The old yogic experts knew a huge number of years before that our bodies are not only material in nature. They are additionally certainly emotional in nature. Science has amassed impressive learning concerning this electromagnetic, bioenergetics working of the human body.

In any case, researchers are first to concede that they don't generally fathom the hidden powers that create life. Logical instruments can look just so far into the issue energy continuum before arriving at their perceptual points of confinement. The extraordinary thing about meditation is that there's nobody size-fits-all arrangement. A few people ponder by sitting unobtrusively in the solace of their home, while others may state that their yoga practice fills in as their meditation. In any case which strategy is utilized, the objective is consistently the equivalent, discover what impacts you and supports you in your development.

1) Guided meditation

Guided meditation is a mix of mesmerizing and representation. It isn't exemplary meditation since it depends on outside improvements, however it is only a stage away from it. The style it uses shifts as it takes the person on an adventure of the faculties and mind to advance relaxing.

2) Chakra meditation

Chakras are a Sanskrit word that implies vortexes of energy. These are essentially energy zones in our body. There are seven fundamental vortexes and they control various parts of our human and psychological lives. A few conventions perceive that, from the medicinal term of the physical body, these seven energy foci are viewed as the endocrine system.

3) Kundalini meditation

Kundalini, which in Sanskrit is followed to the word kundala (which signifies "wound"), over ages came to allude to the inert intensity of profound acknowledgment covered where it counts in the human body, interminably compelled to ascend and show its definitive certainties, power, and rapture. There is a connection among Kundalini and the seven chakran energy.

4) Mantra meditation

Mantra reiteration just means repeating a sentence or gathering of words that have a phonetic noteworthiness. Mantra is inherently identified with sound. Mantra is sound, and sound is resonating in everything in this universe. Present day researchers are starting to perceive as our old sages did, that there exists a vibration which resonates incessantly all through the universe. Models are the sound 'Om' or 'Aum' or even 'I am that I am'.

5) Reiki meditation

Reiki (articulated beam key) is a characteristic healing process that feels like a progression of a high recurrence of energy into and through a specialist, and out the hands into someone else. For all intents and purposes anybody can learn Reiki with no related knowledge or capacity important. The attunement process opens the heart, crown and palm chakras and makes an exceptional connection between the understudy and the Reiki source.

6) Mindfulness meditation

Care is a capacity to focus with a specific goal in mind, deliberately and purpose, focused right now and relinquishing decisions. A few activities that include the training are standing meditation, strolling meditation or eating meditation. The thought stems from this thought: "Any place You Go, Whatever You Do, and There You Are!"

7) Pyramid meditation

Pyramid meditation may have been gotten from the antiquated Egyptians, they utilized pyramids as graves and sanctuaries however they additionally utilized them as approaches to ground and change over vast energies. In the present current world, there are meditation pyramid structures that can be acquired or one can be worked at home by simply utilizing bits of wood and pondering inside.

8) Qigong meditation

Kenneth Cohen deciphers Qigong as "working with life energy, figuring out how to control the flow and dispersion of qi to improve the wellbeing and congruity of mind and body." Such practices have been pervasive in China for 2000-3000 years. The focal thought in qigong practice is the control and control of qi, a type of energy.

YOGA

Practice yoga and be the best surfer that you can be. Each genuine surfer needs to keep up a solid and dapper body and furthermore a quiet demeanour when taking part in such testing game. Surfing educators and specialists state that it's significant not exclusively to be physically adaptable, adjusted and not effectively exhausted, yet in addition to be rationally arranged. Yoga can do much in giving the stamina and mental moulding for surfing.

You may rehearse yoga in various ways. You can try out a class directly in the city and get familiar with the essential yoga aptitudes that can quiet the faculties and improve stance and relaxing. Or on the other hand you can cruise away to an intriguing goal if you have the cash and appreciate a reviving bundle that incorporates yoga, knead, nature climbing, and surfing. Yoga styles differ. A few organizations consolidate the different standards to enable people to have a more grounded, more beneficial and increasingly mollified flow. Individuals leave from a yoga class feeling less focused and on edge and prepared to receive the rewards of a life that is increasingly adjusted.

The intensity of the sea can be overpowering; however, a surfer can remain in direction with legitimate personality moulding for surfing. When you've left on a daring, thrilling get-away and you've enrolled the administrations of a group of specialists to help give an all-encompassing background that incorporates yoga and surfing, you can carry your surfing to the following level.

For apprentices, yoga can be rehearsed a very long time ahead of time before trekking to a surfing spot. By helping to increase parity, dependability, and power, the mind-loosening up action can give you a chance to skim with less exertion and stretch yourself as far as possible with less spills.

Surfing's a game that involves extraordinary physical effort. You need impeccable planning and settle on split-second choices as a wave draws near. In case you're simply beginning, your appendages will throb, and you'll be winded after so much paddling and balancing. The weariness might be sufficient to make the normal individual surrender. A reviving yoga class or loosening up system like Reiki in the wake of surfing can facilitate the pressure and offer profound relaxing.

A yoga ace may direct you through planned activities like 20 minutes of focused postures for the abs and back, about thirty minutes of improving mental center, and a couple of minutes of a loosening up succession to evacuate pressure and impart quiet energy. Through remedial exemplary yoga, you can make a brain, body and soul connection and get recharged moulding for surfing. Most surf and yoga bundles offered by picturesque goals off the beaten track offer solid natural dinners to go with a paramount surfing background and get-away.

One of the most generally rehearsed types of yoga is asana, or stances that link development with breath. Nonetheless, there is significantly more about yoga to investigate past asana; seven different appendages, truth be told. There may come a period in your training where physical postures aren't as basic as what is sprouting inside.

CHAPTER EIGHT

Best Foods To Eat According To Your Chakras

Chakra Foods for Health & Healing

Energy is your basis for all on earth, also in the event that you'll remember from the high school math class, energy can't be destroyed or created; it may simply be altered. Therefore, once you require energy, then you want to eat. But were you aware you could choose foods which have vibrations which match a chakras, so helping raise the resonance's vibration and recharging it? With this knowledge, you could eat for physiological energy and consume to back up your chakras.

Nourishing Energy

Chakras are putting "wheels of light" or energy centers within the human anatomy which start at the root chakra at the bottom of their spine and traveling until the crown chakra at the top of one's face, stopping in five additional things on the road. If your chakras are available and functioning in their own campuses, they draw energy in by the united field that moisturizes and moisturizes your own energy field and keeps you feeling healthy.

The Cost of Imbalanced Chakras

Each chakra functions within a portion of one's own body and distinct regions of one's own life, therefore, if a person is unbalanced, their human body, life, and parts or arenas it controls may become uncontrollable. For example, the heart is attached to the lungs, the circulatory system, along with your own heart, and controls connections along with the own ability to provide and receive love. If your center is twisted, then you might have difficulty keeping healthy connections and may find it hard to permit love in your own life. In the event the chakra stays uncontrollable for long, you might develop physical symptoms such as breathing issues or asthma and may suffer from a heart attack or breast cancer.

The Rainbow Diet: Food to Energy Healing

The fantastic news is you can clean, control, and balance your mind to heal them until physical symptoms develop. That's among the greatest things concerning energy medicine--you also are able to address problems on your field before they manifest inside the human physique. Dealing together with a spiritual teacher or energy system can assist you to figure out what your chakras demands balancing--and a lot of individuals have a few --after which it is possible to aim your efforts regarding the energy centre that really needs the most help. Making the meal choices to the wellness of one's chakras is one other means to begin curing your mind, along with your own life.

A vibrant rainbow diet will probably do a lot more than keep the body healthy -- additionally, it will maintain your chakras healthy. Whether or not you would like to shed weight or boost your energy levels, including foods out of all the colours of the rainbow can allow you to reach balance, and that means that you look and texture your finest.

Root Chakra Food

Your initial Chakra can be found at the bottom of your spine and also can be attached to a survival and security. As your base, your root chakra connects one to the entire system. Whenever your root chakra is, may very well not feel safe within the entire body or become worried.

Ever since this Chakra is about grounding one to the ground, adding origin veggies to your daily diet can greatly fortify your link with the actual world.

Berries

Might Help cure your root canals include beets, rutabagas, ginger, garlic, turnips, onions, onions, and parsnips. Take to them roasted with salt and coconut oil for an effortless mid-afternoon meal that's also yummy!

Protein

Notably, red meat, is additionally abbreviated (believe: epithelial mineral stews and bone broths). If you are a vegetarian or vegan, then green beans and lentils are a wonderful protein source for the root chakra, as are legumes, tofu, along with peanut butter.

Hearty crop grains

Grains for example Bulgar, buckwheat and whole milk, provide the own body with carbs that are complex and so are a very important resource of fiber. While buying sausage in the food store, always go for wholegrains which can be made cereal grains which have the entire kernel. Whenever you are searching for products that are whole, examine the ingredients and be certain the wholegrain are in or close to the surface of the list.

Red fruits

Such as reddish Apples, peas, pomegranates, and berries can help recharge your root chakra.

Spices

Spices such as chives, paprika, and pepper might be inserted to origin chakra foods to get an extra boost of healing.

If you are a tea Drinker, like a cup of rooibos and hibiscus tea (hot or sour) to help treat your root chakra.

Sacral chakra foods

Just below your navel stays the next melody. As the base of one's mental body and the hub of this fun principle, your sacral chakra lets you feel your emotions, to become friendly and open with different men and women, and also to maintain touch with your sexuality and sensuality.

From the sacral chakra, you proceed from looking at the good ground of one's very first spectacle into the liquid world of one's next loaf. This chakra is the gist of life as-found in physiological fluids such as blood and lymph and tears. There's not any life on the planet without water. As the very first chakra challenges one to produce structure and hold the own ground, the second needs one to go which means that your imagination can flow.

A healthful sacral chakra assists in equilibrium and control in your own life.

Plain water

It's the ideal item you'll be able to consume because a sacral chakra curing food.

Clear fluids

Such broth or tea can even help clear and balance the next melody. If you're searching for a few spices for the java, cinnamon and vanilla are all good choices -- and also you can add a little bit of honey to maintain your sacral chakra flowing and fluid.

Berries

That aid cure your sacral chakra comprise peppers, carrots, and so forth. When ingestion sacral chakra veggies, consider adding spices such as garlic, ginger, or simmer to get an additional dose of curing power.

Orange candy foods

Such as melons, mangoes, tangerines, and apples -- can help control your sacral chakra. Along with their own color, these orange fruits have a higher water content that'll help maintain this energy centre flowing and open.

Solar plexus chakra foods

The third chakra is situated halfway between your navel and sternum and is also your supply of yourself and self-esteem. Whilst the furnace of one's own personal power, your solar plexus chakra is dwelling to an own credibility and awareness of self. If it comes to foods for the own solar plexus chakra, you should give attention to foods which greatly alter the vitality from the initial two chakras and ship this up to a fourth chakra.

A healthful and balanced third party seeks to balance self-esteem difficulties and intuition. Bright yellow fruits and veggies help clear and equilibrium your own solar plexus chakra. Think yellow peppers, celery, tomatoes, corn, and peanuts.

Complex Carbohydrates and Wholegrain

Will supply your next chakra with the slow-burning power it ought to convert energy. Avoid foods which your system absorbs fast, such as sugars, white bread, and processed and processed food items. Wholegrain cereals and brown rice are all good alternatives. You might even add flax seeds and sunflower seeds to get fats.

Digestive-friendly foods

These include foods such as kefir, kombucha, and yogurt. They will replenish the good bacteria in the intestine and also keep the energy on your own solar plexus chakra moving.

Chamomile and Herbal teas

Herbal teas (notably ginger and mint) have a calming healing impact in the solar plexus chakra.

Heart chakra foods

Your fourth chakra is situated by your own heart and also is the middle of compassion and love -- both yourself and others. Whilst the bridge between your lower three chakras and top three chakras, the soul is about balance -- getting to balance on your own and along with your own relationships and anything is going on in your ecosystem.

Vibrant green Nutrient-rich veggies

Specially leafy and cruciferous ones such as spinach, lettuces, spinach, chard, bok choy, collard greens, and broccoli, will ramp up the vitality of one's own heart and help heal it. The fourth type is about balance green vegetables have been neither yin nor yang in Oriental medicine, therefore they keep up with the balance that's indispensable to the fitness of this type.

Green water-based alkalizing fruits

Such as limes, green oranges, and avocados, may additionally help balance your own heart chakra so you are able to eventually become more increasingly more mindful.

Green legumes

Consider consuming lima legumes and mung beans. All these may also be curative foods to the heart.

Green-tea

Can help to keep your heart wholesome.

Spices

Such as chamomile, thyme, and ginger helps control your heart.

Throat chakra foods

The fifth chakra is found in the exact middle of one's neck, plus it links the feelings on your heart centre with the notions on your forehead chakra, letting you state your feelings and ideas. Being the very first of this religious metering, the fifth chakra is your portal site by that you bring soul to the physical kingdom, where you join to your true nature.

Representing will, responsibility, power, and sterile throat can attest like a cold or sore throat because of an inability to express oneself. Discussing your truth could be your very best food you can nourish your throat.

Liquids

Like water, fresh 100 percent fruit juices (without the additional sugars), and herbal teas may assist you keep your throat stay healthy.

Blue foods

They may not frequently find these. But blueberries are just one kind of throat chakra healing food that's widely offered.

Fruits that grow on trees

Like apples, peaches, pears, apricots, and plums, also operate to balance the throat.

Third eye chakra foods

The sixth Chakra, known as the brow chakra or perhaps the next eye, is where your master-mind plugs to a fresh sort of wisdom from outside this kingdom, providing excellent insights which may enable one to address almost any issue.

The sixth chakra is situated just above your eyebrows at the exact middle of one's forehead. As the sixth chakra is positioned on mind as opposed to on your chest such as the very first five chakras, it's a somewhat different personality and can be your control centre for a few rather powerful gift suggestions: believing, intellect, psychic abilities, along with intuition. It's really a sensational indigo color, which indicates tranquility and calmness. It's about your intuition, your own skill to plan, prediction, feel, and also understand.

Seeds, legumes, and beans

Notably raw carbohydrates, sprouted almonds, and poppy seeds are nutrient-dense and packaged with anti-oxidants to assist heal your eye.

Water

Metal Detox

Such as harvest grains and mushrooms, work to get rid of heavy metals which come in the own body as a consequence of one's own environment and regular life tasks.

Purple veggies

Just like goji berries, acai, concord grapes, and blackberries supply a megadose of nourishment, maximizing the performance of one's third eye.

Crown chakra foods

The seventh chakra is dwelling to a luminous spiritual centre and connection to Source. Your crown chakra is much significantly more soul than ground, therefore its nutrition comes from sources aside from food, and for example love and also a strong link with the Divine.

The most aspect of one's face, eating foods that are light while participating in a spirit-boosting activity such as meditation may rejuvenate your crown chakra.

Incense and smudging herbs such as sage, copal, myrrh, frankincense, and juniper, may assist bettering your crown chakra to the maximum type of spiritual communication.

The Greatest Guide For Your Chakras: Things to Eat, Say & Want to Balance and Unblock Each

The Root Guide

In equilibrium: feeling safe, secure, and supplied. Possessing a solid feeling of foundation.

Imbalanced: pain or stiffness (particularly in the knees or hips); taking weight in the buttocks or thighs; back pain; distended foot; feelings of bitterness, maybe not remaining safe, along with unmet basic requirements. Flighty personality with a challenging time staying in one place, position, or dating for quite a very long quantity of time.

Supportive meals: Bright reddish foods from the ground (assess sugar content should appropriate), for example crimson apple and cranberry foods together with origins such as radishes, red peppers, beets; red beans and legumes. Red fruits, for example watermelon, pomegranate, cherries, all reddish berries; food increased using profound tree roots or onto a blossom. Red herbal teas like rooibos or hibiscus. Harvest grains along with also other profoundly frozen proteins and grains. Earthly nutrient stews and broths.

Beneficial Strategies: flattening right down to ground by walking bare foot on land, sand, or bud; doing powerful, wrought yoga poses, such as mountain and tree biking. Eating rooted veggies having a focus on the ones which can be reddish or Red Orange in color. Re-establishing roots by understanding how to forgive those mistakes or transgressions given by professionals in early youth and learning how to present those matters that exude an atmosphere of safety, security, and basic demands being met on an everyday basis. Taking ownership of older narrative.

Sayings: I 'm rooted. I'm joking. I'm safe. I'm secure.

The Sacral Guide

In equilibrium: sense of self and other as; healthy connections; disposition or feelings of joy and pleasure; give attention to internal in addition to outside to know balance of both; stability, deficiency of dependence; balanced and healthy reproductive and endocrine system; aesthetically living. Creating wealth.

Imbalanced: addictions, over emphasis on sexuality and self-pleasure, want to squeeze to a particular image, endocrine imbalance along with infertility problems, fighting with the normal aging process, deficiency of self-acceptance, externally moved, creatively stifled. Higher craving for outside stimulation.

Supportive meals: eating what your system requires for optimal wellness and sustenance for example ground and trace minerals; foods having a higher water take into account these; orange foods such as cumin, ginger, garlic, frozen foods using heavy orange, and teas and spices which soothe balance and elimination hormones (calming). Carrots, peppers, squashes, oranges, and tangerines. Foods with vitamins B, C, and A.

Beneficial Strategies: Self-affirmation, playing exactly what the body tells you that it takes. Meditation for equilibrium. Walking, swimming, and slow lifts. Agree feelings of appetite, fate manifesting, and fantasies. Intimate touch.

Sayings: I'm healthy. I'm creative. I'm abundant. I'm composed.

The Gut (Solar Plexus) Guide

In equilibrium: feeling worth things that provide advancement, warmth, and relaxation; proficient in the keeping and setting bounds; sense of self-worth; balanced power that originates from within; healthy gastrointestinal system; trusted sleeping routines; balanced insulin and cortisol levels; skill to listen to gut-feelings. Trust on your own. Intimacy.

Imbalanced: lack of self-worth; sense helpless; many others benefiting from one's energy, personal distance, and celestial presents; salty sleep and digestive routines; sense stress from the nervous system, adrenal fatigue; decreasing in to outmoded sex patterns which don't do the job with you personally; may not readily disperse power; inferior listening habits. Acidic human anatomy. Deficiency of giving eye contact.

Supportive meals: digestive-friendly meals, such as kefir, yogurt, oat bran, cinnamon. Lemon, yellow veggies, and healthful oils and fats. Light green veggies with a superior water-base (celery and pineapple). Melons. Banana, applesauce. Aloe juice. Avocado. Fennel and mint. Soothing rosemary and teas.

Beneficial Practices: meditation, reducing and doing gentle exercises without outside distractions, gut breath-work such as Lion's Breath, and yogic spins. Re-leasing ab muscles.

Sayings: I am worthy. I'm strong. I'm successful. I'm convinced.

One's Center Guide

In equilibrium: loving love. Perhaps not fearful of love. Open. Calm. Willing to keep in touch with the others through one's center. Skill to forgive, comprehending that people are one. Permitting visit to be gift here today.

Imbalanced: Closed heart, feelings of solitude, physical heart or flow difficulties. Fear-induced human body answers. Panic. Tension in torso. Shortness of breath.

Supportive meals: vibrant green leafy vegetables, cruciferous veggies, green water-based leafy vegetables and veggies (such as limes green apples, zucchinis, and celery), transparent water, and healthful fats. Raw nuts. Reduced milk. More avocados. Green beans, lima beans, mung beans. Leafy vegetables. Water.

Beneficial Strategies: deep breath to clean the torso, shoulders pulled down and back to start one's center, lymph heart and torso openers and stretches, and exercises (for instance, extending) that excite the limbic system. Long, slow strikes. Hikes. Swimming. Shoulder and neck massage. Warm baths.

Sayings: I am love. I'm happiness. I'm respectful. I'm receptive.

The Throat Guide

In equilibrium: healthy glands and thyroid, capability to speak the facts, and also to talk to a succinct way. Brevity together with heat. Brand new thoughts.

Imbalanced: G-Land and thyroid difficulties, askew hormonal regulation, inability to talk, skirting across the reality.

Supportive meals: Clear supplements from the ground with water and air elements and, essential, adhering to exactly what the body requires at any moment and giving it just that. Blueberries. Clear fluids or broths. Herbal teas. Alkaline or vitamin water.

Beneficial Strategies: Discussing with brevity. Deep diaphragmatic breath, meditation, rest, getting off things of one's torso. Being in or near the water. Walking out under the huge sky and inhaling oxygen. Visualizing speaking your facts to some family member, friend, or power figure. Being brave. Pictures or graphics of popular bodies of water. Making noises of soothing breeze.

Sayings: I 'm letting go. I'm balanced. I'm honest. I'm free.

The Third eye Guide

In equilibrium: Having the capability to contact information that arises from inside or out, people's sense of oneness with both humanity and the world; an atmosphere of those four facets to be spat together in precision. Greater synchronicity along with ease. Psychic ability. Hearing and visiting significantly more than meets the eyes. Premonitions. Factual fantasies.

Imbalanced: Employing intuition for individual benefit in the forefront of many others, neurosis, anxiety headaches, fictitious god or martyr confusion. Neurosis.

Supportive meals: Water producing foods notably carbohydrates; unsalted nuts particularly peppers; alloy detoxers from the bottom, such as crop mushrooms and grains; purple and purple-red fruits (in tiny amounts), such as for instance goji berries along with vitamin; plums; eggplant; cruciferous veggies specially broccoli; wash organic meats; fish. Pineapple and pineapple.

Beneficial Practices: Meditation; long or yoga stretches; simple repetitive motions like trekking, swimming pool, or taichi; seeing royal arenas which put the increased picture in to perspective.

Sayings: I 'm guided. I'm focused. I'm clear. I'm instinctive.

The Crown Guide

In equilibrium: Energetic and smoothly running physiological shape; the "it" variable; serene, based notions and heartrate; a shine; sense of service; skill to tap into a high intellect and also to easily illustrate what we desire in everyday life.

Imbalanced: Spacy notions or neuroses, migraines, and tingling in nerves and rigid joints, feeling to be lonely and unsupported on the planet, delusions of grandeur.

Supportive meals: water, ethanol or sodium, absorbed through your skin at the high of head/scalp; cleansing blossoms; aloe vera; many different seeds such as chia and citrus; vegetable and bone broths; crucial oils (topical) for unity or equilibrium.

Beneficial Strategies: meditation and favorable idea; requesting for assistance from guides previously and all over, for example family members passed; gratitude techniques; comprehension of breath.

Sayings: I 'm present. I'm here. I'm attached. I'm being.

The Very Best Food To Balance the Body, Mind, And Spirit

A balanced chakra process is really crucial to keep up your general wellbeing: physically, mentally, emotionally, and psychologically. If your chakras are open and balanced, they twist readily and also the vitality flows smoothly throughout the human physique.

One way to maintain those seven major energy centres within tiptop shape is by eating good foods. Eating is not only energy which keeps you moving and up. Since your mind and body are intended to maintain balance, what you may nourish your physical body with, additionally affects your body and chakras.

A balanced "rainbow" diet not merely makes sure your entire body is strong and healthy, but in addition, it keeps your thoughts and soul balanced by nourishing every one of the chakras.

Therefore, what would be the finest food to have pleasure in if you'd like to maintain a healthy diet? There exists an entire selection of options!

Root Vegetables, Red meat For Your Root Chakra

The origin chakra is the power centre that connects one to the aura and it's specialized in survival, security, loved ones, and energy. An imbalance in this very first chakra can make you feeling idle, tired, and worried on your own survival.

Ever since this Chakra is centered on grounding feelings and equilibrium, the ideal cuisine to munch onto nourish it really is origin veggies, like potatoes, beets, ginger, and turnips. Dishes which can be rich with garlic and onion may even be used a lot.

The origin chakra's color is red, therefore, red-colored food may mend blockages within this particular chakra. Some traditional food items that are advocated include red meat, red beans, red berry, ginseng, paprika, cranberries, and some others.

Water, Oranges To Un-block The Sacral Chakra

This chakra is your house of imagination, passion, joy, and heritage. A balanced sacral chakra is going to keep you familiar with your habits and feelings, while still an imbalance will attest into dependence or an aversion for sexual activity, uninspired imagination, very low self-confidence, and reproductive troubles.

Water is a significant component from the sacral chakra, therefore, be certain that you're drinking at a minimum of eight glasses daily!

Any food with high water content is really a great concept, however, as orange is the color of the chakra, you also are able to boost your power more using orange meals, like carrots, squash, apples, and tangerines. Spice-rich chow may even do the job with your sacral chakra, notably garlic, cumin, and ginger.

Soothing, Digestible Dishes To Maintain Your Solar Plexus Chakra Healthy

The solar plexus chakra is responsible for the self, sense of self love, personal ability, and also self-esteem, which means you realize that it's a significant aggravating for maintaining your emotional health under control. Blockages in this particular spectacle will make you feeling useless and helpless, which is mitigated with eating solar plexus favorable meals.

Foods which assist you consume the food are best for your own solar plexus chakra, for example cheese and cinnamon. Additionally, it is a good idea to elect for complex carbs and whole grains regular, rather than becoming packed of an excessive amount of sugars and processed foods.

Organizing your plate with yellowish food may even help, which means you would like consumer more peanuts, yellow peppers, celery, and corn. Slice some lemons up and then drink them. It's refreshing, flavorful, and best for your own solar plexus chakra!

Greens for Your Heart Chakra

The center chakra is the heart chakra, that's that the "hub" of compassion, love, and forgiveness from your system. It's very crucial to keep a balanced chakra system, since it joins both lesser "physical" overlaps together with the three top "spiritual" chakras. After the center chakra is unbalanced, you are going to understand that you're too mad and sour to love someone or you're entirely dependent on the people that you worry for.

This chakra glows green, therefore, root vegetables are the ideal form of food to it. Try out spinach, kale, and broccoli but additionally, there are an assortment options while in the supermarket to select from. Vegetables including salmon and green apples would be also great for your heart, in addition to green tea extract, instead of a substitute for coffee.

Fluids To Open The Throat Chakra

The throat Chakra is devoted to communicating and self-expression, therefore, the fifth chakra is essential that you open your ideas, feelings, and also into the reality. When it's off-balanced, you are going to come to feel ashamed and shy of expressing thoughts and connecting with others.

Liquids, especially water, may help eliminate any problems while in the throat. Fresh fruit juices and herbal teas are all crucial in soothing that chakra too, however, broths as well as other clear fluids additionally get the job done.

The color of this Throat chakra is gloomy, where there are few naturally occurring leafy fruits and veggies that this particular color in character, aside from blueberries. It's believed that berries out of trees will also be excellent choices, like pears and peaches.

Purple Fruits to Tap into Your Third Eye Chakra

The third eye chakra, also known as the brow chakra or even the eye, would be the guts of psychic ability from your system. People tapped into the energy of their next eye routinely have incredible intuition and intellect, in addition to prospect of psychic abilities, such as clairvoyance, precognition, and telepathy.

To assist you balance your third eye, make certain that you eat a whole lot of seeds and nuts, specially almonds and walnuts. Mushrooms, that cleanses compounds, may also be perfect for your own third eye, since they help flush out on heavy metals which are in the human own body.

Water is important to nurture this chakra also, and purple-colored food items, such as eggplant, grapes, and blackberries.

Crown Chakra

The crown chakra, which will be on peak of your mind, joins one to the Divine. A balanced crown chakra is equivalent to enlightenment, letting you call home with usage of boundless wisdom and ability of the Divine.

Because it is that the energy centre that is for this soul of one's inner self in the world, perhaps not plenty of physical foods are supposed to nourish this particular chakra. In reality, eating flaxseed sometimes will reap and replenish the crown.

But water continues to be quite critical to keep this chakra healthy.

Teas to Balance Your Chakras

Most men and women don't believe in maximizing their emotions or energy using tea. However, it is an extremely simple method to raise the kinds of things that you would like in your life or decrease the situations that you never desire. It's possible for you to manage anger, fatigue, stress, and also, you're able to build confidence, imagination, or urge all by simply drinking tea. By understanding which feelings relate to that type, you're able to pin-point that herb which is ideal for you personally through the entire day. Maybe you maintain a natural arsenal in your bag or desk that will assist you while you require it.

As a beginner to the chakras, we'll let you to get to know them just a little better. They have been basically a bundle of nerves which excite certain emotions. You've got seven chief chakras in the system that run out of the bottom of their spine to the peak of your face area. These energy centers may get obstructed for numerous reasons, therefore balancing them is something we all simply keep doing our life. In the event you are feeling off or feel as though you are fighting within a place of life, then you can visit the chakra related to the emotion or region of life you are feeling obstructed and work to balance it.

188

To create the chakra balancing far better, you might even place your goal to develop or discharge a kind of energy since you drink the green tea. You might decide to picture a ball of light that the color of the turning into a wholesome fashion since you drink the tea too. Your thinking may help send more energy into this area and excite the circulation of energy there. There are lots of sorts of air conditioning healing which can be a lot higher priced which demand a power healer emphasizing sending healing energy into a chakras. Even though that's definitely helpful, it is possible to also perform a lot by yourself.

Root Chakra: Dandelion Tea

The Root chakra copes together with all our feelings of safety, our capacity to provide ourselves, using a well-balanced dwelling in addition to energy. If you would like to be grounded and practical in addition to have a solid lifeforce energy, then this tea is able to assist you to trigger this energy centre that's located at the bottom of their spinal column. Dandelion helps detox the kidneys and liver and helps digestion and settles the stomach and reduces muscular strain. Dandelion is employed to generate breast feeding however, not suggested for people who have very low blood pressure. Pain in your back or hip may possibly signify a block inside this chakra. It's packed with vitamin C, nutrients and iron.

Sacral Chakra: Ashwagandha Tea

The Sacral chakra is connected with our familiarity and imagination. It might be connected to dependence as it is jagged. Emotions like shame and anger may obstruct this particular chakra. Additionally, it will be able to benefit you treat mood swings and stress. This chakra might be obstructed if you should be experiencing health difficulties along with your reproductive organs too. Ashwagandha is just a hormone-balancing herb that's also an all-natural aphrodisiac that could help awaken the sexual desire in a person. It's an apoptogenic herb which also makes it possible to feel strong and reduce inflammation in the joints.

Solar Plexus Chakra: Cinnamon Tea

The Solar Plexus chakra is connected with our own motivation, leadership abilities, confidence and sense of humor. When we're shy, hurtful, commanding, competitive, or idle, it's out of balance. In addition, when we've got health difficulties together with your gut such as nausea or vomiting, then it might signal a block inside this chakra. Cinnamon can be a heating system that will help build our internal flame and promote digestion. It's an anti-inflammatory and also a strong antioxidant. It will help control blood glucose and is still a very fantastic source of calcium and fiber.

Heart Chakra: Rose Tea

The Center chakra is connected to our capacity to love ourselves and others. It becomes obstructed once we have been holding despair and despair. When we experience co-dependency or jealousy in addition to being not able to open, there's a block inside this chakra. In addition, health issues linked to the immune system, lungs, heart, and arms may signal a block. Rose is somewhat anti-inflammatory and sedative. Energetically, helps with self-improvement and is famous to help bring love by curing our vibration. It enables you to heal a broken center that you'll be able to experience after losing a stressful life event.

Throat Chakra: Anise Tea

The Throat Chakra allows to get a healthier sharing of thoughts and crystal-clear communication. It enables you to attract your own gifts and talents on the planet. If it's obstructed, we overshare or under share. That could mean that we tell lies and gossip, or people have been vague and passive. Physical medical difficulties with your neck, mouth, neck, and shoulders, indica tea obstruct inside this chakra. Anise is effective for protecting you from unwanted energy that may enable one to either speak negatively or become scared to speak. It's going to help sore throats, coughs, and congestion, in addition to aid in digestion and also lessen the upset stomach.

Third-eye Chakra: Mugwort Tea

The Third Rye Chakra could be your location connected to spiritual wisdom and wisdom. It's connected with an own memory and mental clarity. If you're not able to generate a determination, fight with memory loss, or texture often mistaken, this really is obstructed.

In addition, vision problems, headaches, and ear-aches suggest a block. Mugwort helps open the Third Eye and also certainly will let you look out of your sixth sense. It attracts more active fantasies that will assist you relate with an intuition and can permit one to begin to feel the goals of the others. It frees the creativity and that means you're able to visualize more and relate with healing measurements of understanding. Mugwort additionally helps flow, regulates menstruation, helps calm stress, and enables liver functions.

Crown Chakra: Lavender Tea

The Crown Chakra is connected to feelings to be linked to a spirit and also into the soul realm. It lets you gain access to areas of pure calmness and continue past the fear of passing. Stress, isolation, and emotional health issues frequently suggest a block inside this chakra. Skin problems as well as hair thinning additionally signal a congestion. Lavender is soothing and relaxing, letting you move into a healing vibration. It helps move energy from the lower back into the top triangles so you can experience joy and happiness. It's also fantastic for both PMS, stress, and inflammation.

Chakra Cleansing Herbs For both Empaths and Healers

Energy is your very fabric of life; the building blocks life. When our energy is imbalanced because of scarcity of present-mindedness, minding particular adventures, and repressing our emotions, so we all experience energetic lethargy. Energetic lethargy is similar to stifling the flow of a superior flow, so it turns into a stagnant cesspool of slime and disease.

Energy is intended to flow -- which is its very nature. Whatever blocks which flow creates psychological, physical, and emotional sickness. In reality, you will see that you're feeling that the vibrant and grounded whenever you're earnestly letting yourself have the present moment. That really is our normal condition to be! So, a lot of us fight to have it.

In case you are an energy-sensitive person, like an empath or even healer, you're know firsthand how far distress could end in obstructed energy. Because of stagnant and insufficient energy, you may have undergone (or now feel) the following warnings:

- Chronic muscle injuries
- Weak immune system
- Constant colds and influenza
- Skin problems like acne and psoriasis
- Hormone imbalance

- Headaches and migraines
- Poor blood flow
- Lethargy and reduced energy
- Persistent ailments
- Illness
- Stress
- High blood pressure
- Not enough inspiration
- Irritability and mood swings

If qi or prana lifeforce energy stops flowing, then the chakra or even energy-centers in your own bodies eventually become obstructed. This type of flowing lifeforce energy causes it difficult for all of us to feel rested, focused, energized, and also packed with joy to lifetime. This is the reason why chakra cleansing may be therefore beneficial and useful.

Chakra cleansing herbs for both empaths and healers

You will find lots of chakra cleansing systems on the market, however, certainly one of my favorites would be tea infusions as you receive instantaneous physical, emotional, and energetic advantages.

Not only are herbaceous plants currently an all pure healing option, they are also simple to get. The very best thing is that almost all aura cleansing herbs could be grown in your garden in a relatively minimal priced, and never much hassle.

Listed below would be my best seven chakra cleansing and firming herbs that I would recommend for everybody fighting

194

with imbalanced chakras, & especially empaths, healers, and highly sensitive men and women. If you'd like to have an extensive collection of healing herbs to get empathic men and women, take a look at my empath publication.

The tea firm I urge is known as buddha plus includes a gorgeous variety of teas which are typical natural certified, possess bleach-free totes, and renewable herbs. (Also, just so that you realize, all these are affiliate links and we're going to be given a small commission at no additional cost for you in the event that you opt to buy any. Thank you!)

Inch. Root chakra -- ashwagandha

The root chakra or muladhara accounts to our feelings to be relaxed, secure and sound. In case you have an imbalanced root site, you'll fight with issues such like:

- Feeling disconnected from yourself and many others
- Worries about fundamental needs (food, money, and shelter)
- Never a sense at home anywhere you move
- Persistent anxiety
- Poor flow
- Eating disorders (obesity and anorexia)
- Digestive issues

Ashwagandha, also called Indian ginseng or even cold temperatures cherry, can be a natural herb which has powerful root cleansing properties.

Ashwagandha is really a profoundly nourishing and strengthening herb which reduces stress and helps increase blood flow, alleviates stress and melancholy, as well as has cancer-killing properties rendering it a more highly effective anti-oxidant. This herb also reduces itching, redness cholesterol and diabetes, and also improves fertility.

You can purchase a certified organic tea combination of ashwagandha in buddha teas that's infused with the essence of garnet. On the other hand, you could want to find the suitable package of seven loaf teas for whole playful harmonization.

Sacral Chakra -- Damiana

The Sacral Chakra or even Swadhisthara may be your biggest market of sexuality and imagination. In case you have an imbalanced Sacral Chakra, then you'll experience issues such as:

- Sexual suppression and malfunction
- Emotional repression
- Energetic lethargy
- Not Enough originality
- De-motivation
- Infertility
- Menstrual issues
- Chronic spine pain
- Inability to open to others
- Issue handling feelings
- Coldness and indifference to other people

- Co-dependency and clinginess in associations

Damiana is really a plant native into the United States, Mexico, South America, and the Caribbean, using potent sacral chakra cleansing properties.

Damiana is famous most popularly because of the aphrodisiac impacts that increase sexual interest and performance. But Damiana also offers lots of other benefits like calming the nervous system, reducing stress, and melancholy and controlling glucose.

You can purchase a certified organic tea combination of Damiana specially made for your Sacral Chakra out of Buddha Teas under. Additionally, it is infused with the basis of Moonstone, and it is a wonderful touch! Or you may want to acquire the accentuating package of seven loaf teas for whole inner immersion.)

Solar Plexus Chakra -- Lemongrass

The Solar Plexus (Manipura), may be the biggest market of self and individuality. In case you have an imbalanced Solar Plexus Chakra, then you'll experience symptoms such as:

- Low self-esteem
- Egotism/narcissism
- Insufficient attention and inspiration
- Constant negative self-talk
- Not enough assurance

- Self-isolation
- Stress and melancholy
- Aggression and anger problems
- Poor limits
- Co-dependency
- Pain
- Poor digestion
- Inability to gain or shed fat

Lemongrass is really a common herb frequently utilized in numerous dishes, yet it's significant Solar Plexus chakra cleansing benefits.

With a flavor comparable to lemon (except milder), lemongrass will help reduce melancholy, encourage the immune system, rejuvenate the mind, soothe and cleanse the entire system, improve digestion, and even stabilize cholesterol. Nearly anybody will grow this herb and then crop it to create tea!

If you'd prefer to purchase yours, then you may prefer to try out the certified organic tea combination of Lemongrass out of Buddha Teas. Interestingly, it is infused with the basis of Citrine. It's possible to get yours directly here. (Or, you may prefer to try out the package of seven loaf teas that's an inexpensive option, here.)

Heart Chakra -- Hawthorn Berry

The Heart Chakra (Anahata), is accountable to our capacity to provide and receive love. In case you have an imbalanced heart chakra, then you'll have the following symptoms:

- Resentment and hatred of others
- Not enough satisfying associations
- Stinginess
- Suspicion and paranoia
- Jealousy
- Not enough empathy/cold-heartedness
- Aggression along with being passive aggressive
- Self-victimisation along with martyrdom
- Loneliness and isolation
- Possessiveness
- Grudge-holding
- Melancholy
- Mood-swings
- Sadness and melancholy
- Trust problems
- Heart problems (elevated blood pressure, etc.)

The Heart Chakra is a significant chakra to cure since its thought as fundamental to our own wellbeing and is often called the "Imperial Chakra."

Hawthorn is really a perfect pick for healing heart-centered issues. On its own, Hawthorn Berry features a sweet and slightly sour flavor, nearly similar to sour apple sauce. Hawthorn Berry has long been used in the treatment of heart issues related-to Heart Chakra blockages like angina, arrhythmia, and unstable blood pressure. Hawthorn Berry helps remove bad cholesterol from the blood flow, reduces stress, also it has powerful antioxidant properties which remove free radicals in your system.

You may like to get Hawthorn Berry at a tea combination, like the certified organic box in Buddha Teas that's especially created to your Heart Chakra. This tea combination can be infused with Rose Quartz and can be 100% natural. You'll be able to purchase yours. (Or if you would like to conserve funds, you might decide to try the package of seven loaf teas that is a gorgeous method to immediately stabilize every single loaf.)

Throat Chakra -- Slippery Elm

The Throat Chakra (Vishuddha) may be your biggest market of both self-expression and truth. In case you have an obstructed Throat Chakra, then you'll fight with problems such as:

- Social stress
- Shyness
- Inability to express yourself
- Extortionate inhibition
- Dishonesty
- Miscommunication in associations
- Neck-pain
- Throat Issues

Slippery Elm tastes best if coupled with different herbaceous plants since it's pretty chalky by itself (have a look at Buddha tea mixture). But this tree has significant throat air cleansing benefits.

Slippery Elm is essentially tree-bark out of the Slippery Elm shrub that's grounded to a fine powder. Traditionally, the Slippery Elm was used to cure throat ailments as it functions to gel formerly touching warm water, however in addition, it features a broad array of different advantages. Slippery Elm really helps lubricate the gut and intestines that help treat problems like stomach and stomach disorders. This bark additionally protects the adrenal glands and reduces entire inflammation in your system.

You can purchase a certified organic tea combination of Slippery Elm infused with the basis of Aquamarine directly here. (Or, you could want to find the cheap and suitable package of seven loaf teas for whole Mind Body clearing.)

Third-eye Chakra -- Passion-flower

Your Third-eye Chakra (Ajna), may be your biggest market of intellect, comprehension, and comprehension. In case you have an obstructed Third Eye Chakra, then you'll fight with issues such as:

- Limiting and strict beliefs
- Too intellectual and rigorous focus on logic
- Cynicism
- Residing in a dream universe with no foundation in fact
- Egomania

- Poor attention
- Easily diverted
- Confusion
- Naivety and ignorance's
- Not enough will power and self-discipline
- Reduction in relationship with instinct
- Headaches
- Insomnia
- Obsessive compulsions (OCD)
- Mental disorders like depression and stress

Passion-flower is the perfect herb to the Third Eye Chakra. Passion-flower helps cure insomnia, stress disorders, melancholy, headache, depression, and sometimes even medication withdrawal signs and symptoms.

You may like to get passion-flower at a tea combination, like the certified organic box in Buddha Teas that's especially designed for its Third Eye Chakra. This tea combination can also be infused with Sapphire and can be 100 percent natural. You'll be able to purchase yours! (Otherwise, decide to try the package of seven chakra teas. It is going to help save money.)

Crown Chakra -- Lavender

Your Crown Chakra (Sahasrara), can be the connection with high understanding and spirituality. Should you possess an imbalanced Crown Chakra, you're fight with issues such as:

- Spiritual cynicism
- Apathy
- Self-destruction

- God complex
- Spiritual materialism/addiction
- Dissociation
- Disconnection from fact
- Restlessness and frustration
- Feeling missing
- Existential melancholy
- Loneliness
- Emptiness

Certainly, one of the very uplifting and superbly common air cleansing herbs out there for the Crown Chakra is Lavender.

CHAPTER NINE

Daily Mantra and Affirmations for Manifestation

What Exactly Are Mantras?

Think about mantras as prayers. Whenever you replicate a mantra for yourself, you are engaging your own entire body, mind, speech and thoughts to modify your emotional condition.

After just a bit of practice, this might enable you to attain a deep level of attention, anyplace, and anytime. If you are motivated to test some out yourself, have a look at my guide to mantras for serenity.

Mantras are much more than only a physical practice. They could permeate your mind, changing your inner psychological condition just as far as your outer body.

Afterward, in this guide, you will learn that the sounds of the chakras.

All these are well known as bija mantras:

Bija mantras (significance seed from English) focus your time and concentration towards your own mind, so you are able to trigger and raise the flow of energy throughout the entire body.

204

Therefore, since you have a better understanding of chakras and mantras, let us consider just how and why they need to be united in spiritual practice.

Benefits of Chakra Mantras

Just how do Chakra Mantras increase the level of one's lifetime? The advantages of practicing mantras

- Boosting the human mind role: bettering your mind with mantras can cut the results of aging, and via your memory, focus and health.
- Mental-health: Reduce your stress levels, treat melancholy/stress, and also gain greater introspective insights to the way the mind works
- Physical Health: from relaxing and finding greater calmness with mind, you might lessen the dangers of elevated blood pressure, Alzheimer's and spine pain
- Self-development: using more inner calmness includes more self-control, subject and comprehension of the way you're feeling.
- Relationships: after you've attained a deeper degree of introspective insight, then you are going to be joyful and aware of how your actions affect the others. This in turn enriches your own relationships, interactions and capability to communicate.

Just how Do Chakra Mantras Work?

To start, just locate a quiet spot to relax and meditate, when you chant to yourself the chakra mantras I have detailed below.

There is a distinctive mantra to replicate for every single quadrant -- understood like a bija or "noise of this chakra." Whilst chanting you'll have noticed that the vibrations flow throughout the own body as energy which triggers every single quadrant. This replica will also improve your own concentration.

I have included an overview of every chakra, to ensure you know very well what each disc is accountable for. You will also find hints about the best way to pay attention to exaggeration e.g. to your crown chakra, you should imagine drifting away out of this material, physical universe that the majority of people feel attached to.

Your disposition mantra practice ought to be balanced:

Since you'll find under, although it's crucial that you trigger the air, an excessive amount of energy flow can trigger a poor effect too.

Use these mantras as being a means to balance your time flow -- in order your chakras are blocked over compromised.

Chakra Mantras to Try out

If you practice these mantras, you are ostensibly planting a seed to your own chakra.

All the Chakra mantras make vibrations, together with everyone built to especially cure a specific mantra.

All these seeds are referred to like a bija.

As an example, the LAM headline opens your Base Chakra, whereas chanting HAM will make vibrations for curing the Heart Chakra.

LAM for Muladhara that the Bottom Chakra -- Earth Element.

The LAM chant conquer your Base Chakra. Therefore, just how can this Base Mantra Chakra assist you?

- The Muladhara origin chakra is connected with our own instincts
- It is all about how we connect to your outside universe -- communities, loved ones, friends, and connections
- This links to some instincts like joy, pain, and heritage
- Should you ever be feeling a good deal of fear and worry, this chakra is frequently the main reason
- Practicing Base chakra mantras will boost your awareness of security, stability, and over all degrees of stress.

VAM for Swadhisthana that the Sacral Chakra -- Water Element

Interestingly, that the sacral chakra is closely connected to emotions such as self-confidence, self-esteem, self-worth and also your general awareness of imagination.

Here's a couple of additional matters which you ought to know concerning any of it:

- When your sacral chakra is blocked, then it can result in issues with violence, joy along with dependence
- Emotions like innocence, imagination and willingness from the sacral
- An amalgamated sacral chakra can result in you feeling isolated from the others round, inducing sexual energy and struggling with societal skills
- Over the reverse side, if your chakra is over charged, you could have trouble with dependence, over-sexualised thoughts and perhaps even obsessive tendencies

RAM for Manipura that the Solar Plexus Chakra -- Fire Element

RAM is your Chakra headline for its Solar Plexus. Therefore, how can the solar plexus impact you?

- Adrenal glands cells in your liver, your metabolic process along with your digestive capacities are affected by the wellbeing of your own solar plexus chakra

- On account of the digestive connections, this really is a really instinctual chakra e.g. your gut instinct. If you are feeling something is incorrect, or just like you are not creating the Ideal choices, are connected to the chakra
- How we think of ourselves and our own internal self comes stems out of the solar plexus
- Emotions like guilt and shame may obstruct this particular spectacle, therefore, it is essential to be proud of yourself and that you're

YAM for Anahata that the Center Chakra -- Air Element

This chakra is at one's center, along with the headline is YAM.

Because of the connections into one's center, this is really actually a chakra for compassion and love.

If your chakra is balanced, you're feeling approval, empathy for others, compassion, warmth and love to all those around you. If you are struggling with melancholy or societal stress, it can be as your Anahata chakra is obstructed. This may result in feelings of solitude, or maybe jealousy.

Additionally, an imbalance in this center chakra may cause problems with blood pressure, respiratory troubles, and also a physical disturbance from the muscles.

Whilst chanting the chakra mantra Yam, strive to concentrate on feelings of warmth, love and empathy.

Focus on this people you are thankful for in your own life.

HAM for Vishuddha that the Throat Chakra -- Akasha Element

The throat chakra headline is HAM. It is tightly connected with communicating and how we express ourselves on others.

Hormones, from the thyroid gland, are all made out of within this spectacle, therefore, that it's crucial to continue to keep it balanced to get psychological equilibrium.

Exactly why is this an essential chakra?

- Since we communicate and speak with ourselves on other people through our throat
- Our remarks our ideas and the way we handle others largely stems from your Throat Chakra
- This may also alter whether we stay up for itself and also, we make decisions whilst conveying with other people
- This chakra is responsible for displaying hope, generating bounds, expressing ourselves, and producing conclusions

KSHAM for Ajna that the Third Eye Chakra -- Mahatattva

KSHAM is your mantra for the next Eye. When practicing this mantra, attempt to concentrate on shattering your Truth about the Earth, and creating greater emotion out of the own perspective.

210

So, what's that the Third eye chakra connected to?

- The third eye is related to the pineal gland, which produces melatonin for resting and sleep
- This additionally produces dimethyltryptamine -- a more potent psychedelic hallucinogen naturally manufactured inside your own body
- This Chakra is connected to psychic discovery -- for example your own instinct to get prospective events, vision, and outlook
- As soon as your next eye is obstructed, it's often right down to an illusion of these. If we cannot find out that which we actually are -- or exactly what life actually is -- subsequently triggering the third eye chakra will assist
- This can also lead to feelings of insomnia, exhaustion and disillusion
- When you've too much energy concentrated on the Mahatattva, then you might fight to focus, texture delusions or suffer from headaches

AUM for Sahasrara that the Crown Chakra

AUM is your chakra mantra with this particular energy tip. Whilst replicating this particular headline, attempt to focus on attention your time , to the peak of your face. Let yourself float freely far from this material, physical planet and alternatively interact together with all the energy flow on the market.

How will assessing the Sahasrara chakra change how you are feeling?

The Shasrara is a very introspective chakra, connected with intellect along with your spirit:

- It is on the power flowing in your entire body, releasing a bunch of vitality out of the very surface of your mind (the crown)
- It may help to envision a pool of white light, flowing out of the mind all of the way to your feet -- radiating energy through the human entire body.
- The crown chakra is accountable for religious vitality, also disposition. It enriches our consciousness, our view of this world as well as our motto as a connected being. If you are overly attached to the bodily universe, or if you are an honourable individual, you are in danger of obstructing your crown chakra.
- Symptoms of an obstructed crown chakra comprise sense covetous, inducing religious comprehension, cynicism and being greedy
- Should you've too much power flowing into the particular spectacle, you may feel isolated from the physical universe, exhausted, or even lacking curiosity about everyday life

Strategies to get using chakra mantras

- Below are some tips in order to understand and properly utilize mantra:
- Do not attempt to do everything at the same time.
- When you are chanting chakra mantras, only concentrate on a single chakra at the same time. This gives you a higher amount of attention on every chakra, focusing your recovery energy throughout your system.

- Show patience
- Chanting mantras is incredibly enabling, but do not expect results every moment.
- Developing peace within requires years of consistent training, and it's really no different using chakras. If you opting to get daily, you wouldn't be expecting you'll eventually become knowledgeable right away.
- It is exactly the same for chakra mantras -- simply take time and revel in the journey.
- It is all from the timing
- In case the mind is busy, diverted and maybe not entirely concentrated on the task at hand, you won't have the ability to discover inner serenity.

Therefore, you need to locate a handy time to rehearse these chakras, once you are relaxed, serene and willing to focus your entire attention.

Here is what I encourage:

- Devoting a particular time of this afternoon to practice
- Pull the plug on all gadgets so that you aren't distracted by noises and alarms
- Frequently, early mornings and evenings are the perfect time for you to rehearse chakra mantras
- Make certain nobody is going to burst in the room when you are practicing. So, ensure privacy.
- Hunger will distract you! Eat something healthy and light before beginning
- Wear the proper clothing

To realize quicker quantities of comfort, you have to become comfortable. So, here are some tips to ensure you are comfortable for practicing mantras:

- Dress in something which will not leave you feeling overly hot/cold
- Make sure that your clothes are breathable and maybe not overly tight fitting
- Do not wear something which is going to confine your flexibility. Tight jeans really are a lousy idea!
- Robes are often a favourite option for chanting chakra mantras.

Seven Affirmations to Balance your seven Chakras & Nurture Greater Self-acceptance:

1. Crown Chakra: I'm filled up with greatness.
2. Third eye Chakra: I'm shrewd.
3. Throat Chakra: I'm learning, and I will be growing. We are growing and learning.
4. Heart Chakra: I really love and love myself because I'm.
5. Solar Plexus Chakra: I accept myself completely. I accept I have strengths, and that I accept that I've flaws.
6. Sacral Chakra: I'm both strong and sensitive.
7. Root Chakra: I'm full of humility. I'm enough as I'm.

Seven Chakra Affirmations for Growing Trust:

1. Crown Chakra: I let it head, and that I hope that the practice of life.
2. Third eye Chakra: I'm a smart decisionmaker.
3. Throat Chakra: I'm full of the strength of soul.
4. Heart Chakra: I'm full of courage.

5. Solar Plexus Chakra: I admit that I will be growing and learning.
6. Sacral Chakra: I'm balanced. I understand when to behave, and that I understand when to hold back.
7. Root Chakra: I'm disciplined.

Chakra balancing is an essential tool for tapping into the authentic self. Experience the energy, confidence, and power that comes out of balancing and aligning each one your chakras--also observe what goes on!

CHAPTER TEN

How to Increase Your Life Force Energy

The Breathing Process

To inhale is to get life power, and to exhale, our very own energy. Great breathing carries with it most extreme energy through least exertion. The vast majority don't inhale appropriately. A total cycle of breathing is worked in three stages. At the principal stage, the solar plexus and the stomach ascend, as we push out our tummy and fill our lungs with air. Placing your hands on the stomach, to check its developments, is prescribed. The lower part of the lungs is topped off, first, at that point the lung's center part, and right a short time later the upper part. At the subsequent stage, we stop the relaxing for five seconds - that is the time required for the essential energy, which is noticeable all around, to arrive at the platelets. Short breathing would not pass on to the blood its essence. The more we keep the air in our lungs, the more wellbeing and energy we get. In the wake of holding our breath, exhaling is done considerably more proficiently. At the third stage we exhale the air through the nose, in a very inverse manner to the inhaling process. We push the ribs with the neckline bone downwards and push the gut muscles internal to exhale all the trapped air. These activities ought to be performed normally, without power.

Breathing is a characteristic process, without strain and exertion. The most ideal approach to practice it is by lying on the floor - and the jaw held forward, so as to fix the spine. Researchers have discovered that during full, profound breathing, the mind emanates progressively alpha waves, and that causes relaxing. Ten minutes of conscious, deep breathing, fills us with energy and tranquility. It is an activity that dissuades strain and fear. By holding our breath, cells get more oxygen, on account of the more drawn out span of contact with the air. We may see through visionary vision, that during the time the breath is held, a tremendous measure of prana is spread in the body – that never happens when we don't hold our breath. An increasingly proficient approach to hold our breath is by moving the sphincters (the rear and the frontal sphincter).

When we are moving the sphincters, we contract our stomach too, and that helps particularly the breathing process. It is constantly advised to pull the stomach inside while exhaling. The breathing ought to consistently be done through the nose as the air heats up, along these lines destroying contrasts of temperature, between the body and nature. The hairs of the nose additionally channel out residue and earth particles that may cause aggravations. Air incorporates nitrogen, oxygen, and Prana - life's energy. These components are blended with one another; however, prana can go through dividers, and is found all over. There is no spot without prana. To get it by breathing is basic. We hold prana in a few structures:

- Through the tips of the nose's nerves.
- Through the tongue which uncovers the preference for nourishment - and that is the reason biting is so significant.
- Through the skin in remaining under the daylight.
- Through breathing through the air.
- Through the eyes.
- Through representation and focus. These increase the amount of the prana.

Prana complies with the expression of ideas. When breathing is under conscious control, we can hold more prana.

The majority of the psychological healers accentuate the significance of breathing, in profound advancement. Charging the blood of oxygen and prana is a key to modify and mend the physical body. When we don't inhale accurately, damages accumulate, the body's vibration diminishes, and there is a negative effect on body and soul. While we develop, we neglect to inhale appropriately. Shallow breathing, just with the development and compression of the lungs, without the development of the stomach, doesn't permit relaxing.

In each breath that we take, the universe conveys air into us, and siphons it back when we exhale it. Breathing discloses to us that we are a piece of the soul that works everything. In Buddhism, the beat of breathing is being utilized to grow the outskirts of the ego. When you inhale, attempt to know the all-inclusive energy - and do express gratitude toward it, for vitalizing each cell in your body - and you will get the world
218

inside yourself. When you exhale, send your thank you, your energy, to all the enduring individuals. Consequently, you get life by inhaling, and you give from yourself by exhaling. Inhaling speaks to the likelihood to get, and exhaling speaks to the giving up, the giving, and carries with it relaxing. Breathing is a common component to both body and soul. It is an activity that widens our consciousness. It is a great idea to envision that the air climbs along the spine, when we exhale, and slide along it when we inhale.

The air we inhale makes certain movements inside us, and afterward gets out. We should give it a chance to get out. If we won't exhale the air, we would not have the option to get new and natural air. If we wish to get during our lives, we need to give. If we include or kept inside ourselves feelings of anger, of aspiration, or negative emotions, we can give them a chance to be released by the activity of exhaling. Along these lines, we empower life energy to flow inside – while the poisons are, being let out of the body. So as to get the grandiose energy – the widespread power – we need to inhale intentionally, to inhale the light and the excellence and to cast out by exhaling the fiendishness, the illness, and the fear. We are breathing deliberately when with each inhaling, we connect with the universe, and with each exhalation, we send light and love to the earth.

To inhale appropriately, the spine must be straight. It is possible to see the body's degree of energy through the stance of the chest. Emotional pressure makes the chest solidify.

219

Negative emotions solidify the chest, which causes breathing issues and absence of energy. We should treat the solidified chest, loosen up the emotions (a psychological process), and work on the chest's stance (a physical process). The chest will permit the passage of substantially more air, and more energy, when it is adaptable and discharged. A "shield" in the chest territory, or the solar plexus, demonstrates that the individual is loaded with wrath, and expects to do brutal action. At that point, issues of stomach, respiratory system or the liver and nerve bladder may reveal themselves.

Conscious breathing empowers legitimate meditation and decidedly impacts our wellbeing, while concentration on the entry of air through the nostrils brings more prana to the body. We more often than not inhale twelve times each moment; during meditation we inhale multiple times or even less every moment - yet in a lot further way. During meditation, we loosen up the body. At the point when the body is loose, there is a decent progression of energy if there have not been blockages for an long time. When we focus on our breathing, daily issues are overlooked, and intrusions of the external world disappear step by step – while this movement calms the thoughts and empowers us to tune in to our body. In the event that we focus on a specific thing, and get eager, or if we feel a forceful passionate fervor or fear, we quit relaxing. When we start breathing, once again, we for the most part quickly swallow the air. Fundamentally the same thing happens when we eat excessively quick. The outcome is gas and stomach-aches. In this manner, it is essential to show ourselves how not to quit breathing, and how to inhale appropriately.

Breathing mirrors our state of mind, and equally it may change our mind-set. When we are upbeat, we inhale deeply, and when we cry, the body is twisted, and we take in short and sporadic breaths. Power over breathing empowers authority over emotions.

As per Dr. Drunvalo Melchizedek, an etheric direct exists in the body for the progression of Prana inside us - it is two inches in distance across, its length from eight inches underneath our feet, up to somewhere in the range of eight inches over our heads. Man used to inhale from the outset through that channel, while concentrating the energy of the earth and the universe in a certain chakra. In such a breathing process, the prana would go through the pineal organ and actuate it. The pineal organ would get the energy and circulate it all through the body. This organ connects us with the binding together head of the universe. Today, in view of changes in the breathing process, we don't utilize that organ any longer. It did shrink and we presently get the duality of the universe rather than the solidarity. Dr. Melchizedek prescribes breathing and engaging the prana from the universe and the earth through the etheric channel, gathering it from the start in the solar plexus, later in the Heart's chakra and from that point transmit it into the emanation. The prana radiation in addition to unlimited love elevate us to higher circles.

Why we prescribe to inhale further and all the more gradually? In the event that we inhale gradually, we can avert anger. Anger and fear, which cause pressure, accelerate the breathing process in an undesirable manner. Including when there are feelings of fear and stress, we should inhale appropriately. Especially during stress periods, we should inhale gradually - the propensity for counting up to ten preceding any further advance helps in instances of pressure. Fear when all is said in done and stage trepidation might be defeated through moderate relaxing. We inhale around ten to twelve times each moment. When we take in a shallow way, we decline the ingestion of energy, and we don't broaden the lungs' volume. The result is firm lungs; and thus, deep breathing would be uncommon and difficult to perform, and out of the accessible energy we would utilize just a little part. At the point when pains attack us, we need to inhale profoundly and focus on the breath, not the pain. This sort of movement doesn't dispose of the pain but can lessen it.

Focus reinforces everything on which we concentrate. That is the reason it is a great idea to figure out how to focus on breathing, not the pain. Without air loaded with particles we can't endure. The particle's state is a state, wherein the dynamic molecule may give or get an electron. Positive particles effectively retain electrons and negative particles are prepared to give electrons. It is charming to inhale almost a cascade or in a woodland or just after a storm - when the quantity of negative particles noticeable all around is high. Then again, before a storm we feel a substantial burden noticeable all around, due to the colossal number of positive particles in it. At home, the circumstance isn't perfect for solid breathing, because of the incredible measure of electronic gadgets, for example, TVs, PCs, radios, including rugs, curtains and fabrics made of manufactured material, which produce positive particles. In the modern era, the measure of negative particles in the city is decreased as these particles hold fast to clean, smoke scents and tobacco, and tumble to the ground. The convergence of negative particles increases our sharpness, hinders the breathing process and realizes a positive feeling, helping our focus. The air that we for the most part inhale is stacked with a negative burden, whiles the air that we exhale is stacked with emphatically charged carbon oxide.

We suggest utilizing an ionizer which cleans the sullied air in workplaces, homes, cars, and particularly, smoking zones. It is essential to know about the way that the atmosphere contains particles, similarly as the body is made of iotas. The electrons are particles of light, and inside our body the progression of negative particles inside the cells, blesses us with life - because of the digestion and the breathing process.

Breathing links body and soul as it is the body's just programmed capacity that can be effectively changed through conscious will. Breathing brings oxidation and empowers organ function. Do the inhaling through the nose and imagine that it is done through the arms and legs and the Root chakra. Carry the air to the hara region. Every one of those breathings, which gather much energy at the hara, may invigorate fervor and even tremors – if the energy isn't utilized toward the part of the arrangement. The energy is dispelled by envisioning how it circles multiple times the navel clockwise, and multiple times the other way, counter-clockwise – that is, the means by which it works with men, and the other way around with ladies. This breathing brings energy everywhere throughout the body. With training, you can learn through perception to inhale through the bones, the skin or any organ for strengthening.

Incomprehensible Breathing

While inhaling, draw the tummy inside and contract the solar plexus, which moves descending and makes weight on the organs in its region. Simultaneously the energy is being moved to the meridians. While exhaling, enlarge the volume of the stomach region, by blowing up the belly. The process is inverse to common relaxing. Essence tops off the hara zone. This sort of breathing is utilized while rehearsing Chi-Kung and Tai Chi. Yoga educators guarantee this is the correct method for relaxing.

Cooling Breathing

We load the body with positive energy by breathing; we quiet it and loosen it up. It is possible to heat up or to cool the body, by breathing and focusing on it. It is possible to change the prana – the grandiose energy, into a feeling of warmth or cool, as per the condition of inhaling. Inhale deeply with legs joined and envision that with each breathe the air is cooled. Similarly, you can heat up the body, yet most importantly you should gather in an exceptionally little piece of the body. Another technique to cool the body is by reaching out a piece of the tongue - a large portion of an inch – and collapsing it into a U shape, similar to a bow. The breathing is done through the tongue while it is in the state of a sickle; we at that point hold our breath and exhale through the nose. The air in conventional breathing enters through the nose and makes warmth in that manner; while in this technique, it enters through the mouth and makes coolness. Taking along these lines accelerates digestion and has great effect on the eyes, ears, and the liver.

Breathing Through the Energy Centers

Breathing through the energy centers is possible and breathing through the solar plexus or the hara center is recommended explicitly. The breathing is performed through the lungs, however, simply envision that it is done through the energy centers. You may inhale the sun's energy or the world's energy.

The technique depends on a hypothesis' case that energy is coordinated to everywhere, by idea and the correct practice. Put your hands on the main energy focus while you envision when inhaling the red shading. Feel how the inside is topped off with vivid prana when you hold your breath – and afterward, exhale. Do it a few times with each energy focus, and its correct shading. Toward the end, so as to link the energy centers one to the next, envision that you inhale the prana from your feet to the main energy focus, and a short time later, from the principal focus to the subsequent one, etc. through every one of the centers.

An Additional Exercise

It is a blend of breathing activities with representation. You should attempt to find in your imagination how the air enters the body. Feel how it flows inside your body, and warms you, how it fills the body's organs. Envision that with the air the heavenly love, which is all over the place, enters in your body. When you hold your breath, feel how it fills each cell in your body. While exhaling, send forward your hands, with broadened and open fingers and feel how you emanate love to the universe. It is a great idea to envision that each breath joins you with the universe. After the breathing activities, it is a lot simpler to feel the progression of energy - the warmth, the sensitive feelings and vibrations in the arms.

A Breathing Exercise That Loads the Body with Energy

Inhale and envision the energy consumption. Inhale, hold your breath and maintaining in mind that exhaling, send the energy by representation to the agonizing territory or organ through your hands. In the second time that you hold your breath, feel as though the energy is entering the excruciating organ. Breathing activities with perception are utilized for healing. Seeing the natural air that transmits the energy to the blood, in an individual's imagination - is very attractive. Feel how the activity is accomplished in the body. When you are inhaling, envision your contemporary state – your damaged cells for example; and when you hold your breath, think about the message and the image that would actuate the cells of a particular organ. Somewhere in the range of three seconds are typically satisfactory for it, however, time may be extended. At that point, request the capacities to be done while exhaling, imagining how the breath dives deep into every cell of the harmed organ.

When inhaling the counsel is to "welcome" the light, "breath" the light; and keeping in mind that exhaling to send it to the organs, to some harmed region, or to the universe. Focus on the light and send it to everybody. Along these lines, you discharge a solid psychological energy that raises the human awareness. It is critical to recall that common breathing is normal and programmed and is managed with no effort. The activities are an instrument that causes us to arrive at the correct method to relax. Profound and appropriate breathing can improve our wellbeing, correct our feelings, and carry with it positive feeling, relaxing, and significant serenity. It would be a pity, not to exploit such a basic and regular process that has inside it such huge numbers of potential outcomes.

Food

With appropriate nourishment, we add a very long time to our life; with terrible nourishment we abbreviate our life. The nourishment we eat affects our physical and psychological wellness. Truly we are what we digest, as each cell in our body is made from the sustenance we eat. Awful wellbeing is the result of three principle

Factors:

1. Collection of toxic substances in the body, as a result of an ill-advised diet
2. Absence of supplements as a result of eating prepared and rationed food.
3. Stress and negative musings and feelings.

Nourishment Absorption

Numerous individuals don't know that absorption begins in the mouth. The stomach related process begins with the smell, the sight, even the idea of food. Hence, it is imperative to masticulate the food well, grind it into minor particles, and accordingly facilitate the absorption process. Like the human body, food also has biochemical and electromagnetic energy, and chewing discharges the energy inside of it. As per Indian meditation, we need to chew our food thirty-two times. The point is to process the sustenance and transform it nearly into a fluid, and after that to swallow it. The act of chewing activates salivation, which helps absorption. It isn't advised to eat and drink simultaneously, however, to drink between meal, plain water would be the best. It is prescribed to have sustenance in its dry structure, since drinking fluids with eating nourishment weakens the gastric fluids.

When we are anxious and eat excessively fast, we don't process appropriately. Before eating inhale deeply a few times and loosen up the body, feel the congruity that exists among you and the nourishment and offer thanks, as it is acclimated in various religions. As indicated by the assessment of dietitians, adjusted nourishment is made out of half - 60% starches; 20% protein, which is significant for tissue development and support; 30% of fat - separated into 20% of unsaturated fat and 10% of saturated fat. A protein-enhanced dietary plan negatively affects absorption, and furthermore, irritates function of the heart and kidneys. Absorbed fats cause blockages. It is in this manner prescribed to diminish the utilization of domesticated animal's items, meat and entire milk, which contain saturated fat. Our body reminds us of the mechanics of a vehicle. The starches and the fat are the body's fuel and oil, however without the electric spark - the energy, the vehicle won't begin. To our lament, individuals tend their cars more than their own bodies. They never put water rather than fuel in their vehicle's tank, however, they continue eating processed foods, which incorporates extra fixings that the body can't process. The body can adapt as long as it has a reasonable hold of energy and proteins, yet insusceptibility doesn't keep going forever.

To ease processing, it is prescribed not to blend strong sustenance of various supplements. In this way proteins (meat) ought not to be blended with starches (batter and bread). Organic products ought to be eaten crisp, and we should hold up twenty - thirty minutes before eating whatever else. It is smarter to prepare the meal directly before gobbling it up, in light of the fact that continued heating up of food and continued cooling in the fridge - diminishes its sustaining worth. With respect to sweet nourishments, they ought to be totally relinquished (aside from nectar), also industrialized sustenance, which contains substance fixings. Bugs are more effective than men. If we have for example two packs of flour, - crude flour, and white flour – the bugs will favor the crude flour that contains minerals.

All Encompassing Healing

All-encompassing healing means re-establishing wholeness and blessedness in the physical and unpretentious bodies. The individual is a little molecule in the gigantic general field. A conscious individual who knows about the unity of the fiery fields is freed from the deception that there is only a physical world in presence. Truth be told, each person is in real touch with the universe. In any case, as a result of problem and turmoil occurring in his very own vigorous fields, the awareness of man is obscured for a long spell of time. Therefore, he overlooks his feeling of solidarity with God. The vast majority are not conscious that a lively issue exists at the base of each physical issue. So as to treat the issue, we should change the quality and measure of energy, which flows in the vivacious systems.

Our frame of mind to life impacts the manners in which we adapt to issues, both physically and mentally the same. If we live in oneness with the inestimable laws, we can be sound. Each illness carries alongside it a message and a chance to learn and realize ourselves better. We should not fear from attempting to alter what is to be corrected. That is the reason each illness is in a manner our very own meditation inside states. Contamination of the blood as come about because of eating processed sustenance's, breathing unclean air and introduction to stress conditions are additionally at the foundation of our sicknesses.

Malady is a biochemical and electromagnetic dis-request of the cells in the body. It is brought about by negative feelings and it is a side effect of protection from change. The treatment of the indication alone doesn't fix the malady, on the grounds that there is a more profound reason for the ailment. Illnesses are the body's preliminary to dispose of toxin. This is the reason behind why it is great to give the side effect a chance to convey what needs be drastically. We should experience the manifestation, with no emotional judgment or any displeasure. We should treat it with self-examination and with the information of the progression of energy in the body. In the event that the parity in some part has been irritated, the entire living being is influenced right away.

Wellbeing is in actuality a declaration of the concordance between various types of energies. The healer transmits an electromagnetic charge that arranges, balance off toxic substances, and brings wellbeing. A healer and a sensible or wise man have an excess of prana - the inconspicuous energy in charge of the body imperativeness, while a wiped-out man experiences prana shortage.

There are a few phases in healing:

1. Checking if the treated patient gets the healing energy with euphoria.
2. Diagnosing the quality.
3. Refining the emanation.
4. Energy transmission from the healer to the treated patient.
5. Treating the Chakras, balancing the energy and the meridians

The significance of profound breathing and a casual state are fundamental during the transmission of the healing energy. With right handed individuals the left hand as a rule gets the energy - for the most part the healer lifts the left hand upward to get infinite energy. The dynamic right hand emanates the energy and accordingly he holds it toward the patient air or the treated organ. With left-handed individuals, the activity is a remarkable inverse. Energy may be obtained, coordinated or transmitted also through two hands. Healing can be constrained by the desire of the healer by means of idea and the healer can send energy with two hands.

The extraction of foul energy as well as expansion of filtered energy -delivers healing. The reason for some infections is an absence of energy. Where there is a deterrent, there is additionally an amassing of energy, an obstacle of the flow and that hindrance must be discharged. The healer ought to consistently have the patient's affirmation to treat him. The best perspective to transmit and get energy is the point at which the mind conveys alpha waves – the condition of relaxing. The healer must be in a condition of congruity with the patient, so as to transmit energy proficiently.

There is no utilization in the transmission of energy before refinement of the emanation. Electricity produced via friction, which holds fast to the atmosphere, averts the attainability of energy transmission. This is the motivation behind why the quality is constantly cleansed before any transmission of energy. In treating certain organ, or a specific spot in the body, it ought to be first cleansed. Filtration much of the time makes a nice feeling. New age meditation uses vibration methods. At the point when these processes are consolidated, they increase enormously the power of the energy.

CONCLUSION

In order to address a contortion in our chakras and accomplish chakra healing, we have to loosen up profoundly. Any internal image that assists relaxing with preferring a bloom opening out from the chakra or an influx of water flowing in and out from the chakra will relinquish any sort of contortion that has developed in the chakra. In any case, we ought to know that chakra opening is first an occasion of the mind and just optionally of the body. It is our restricting convictions and mentalities that have caused every one of the issues in our chakras. Thus, we ought to be set up to take a look at these expressions and afterward let them go.

An excellent mix of herbaceous plants for every single quadrant can be found through Buddha teas. If you would like to approach your healing at a systematic manner, focus using a single chakra weekly. Enjoy it and contain yoga poses which aim each chakra in addition to crystals and colors. This focused approach can truly assist you to find the impacts happen and undergo profound healing. Whenever you experience an aim for every week, you have to come to new realizations on your thought patterns and determine what you're able to shift. This enabling exercise can be put into place without quitting everything on your own life too. You're able to shell out just a bit of time daily on healing and begin to become a positive person.

You can create monthly a practice of healing and determine just how much progress you make. Consider just how to add nutrition and health in your chakra unblocking. Possessing some curative remedies such as Reiki, massage, or consistent baths, together with a fantastic assortment of nutrition in your daily diet may help. Turn to food items which help each quadrant in the event you need also; it'll enable your healing process. The outcomes are going to be astonishing as whenever you focus your power and mind to the desirable results, you push it, using the ability of this Universe. Bear in mind that, whenever you concentrate on love, the more your whole being starts to become one and your own life is going to likely be infused with that.